Houghton Mifflin
Math

D0878528

Grade 5

Adequate Yearly Progress
Assessment Guide

Adequate Yearly Progress Tests

Practice Tests

Answer Key and Scoring Rubrics

 HOUGHTON MIFFLIN

BOSTON

Contents

What Is NAEP?

NAEP, the National Assessment of Educational Progress, is also known as "the Nation's Report Card." It is a continuing assessment of "what students in the United States know and can do." Since 1969, NAEP assessments have been carried out in various content areas, including mathematics at grades 4, 8, and 12. While NAEP does not provide scores for individual students or schools, it gives results about subject-matter achievement for populations of students based on sample populations. NAEP assessments allow the comparison of students in one state with students in other states and with the nation as a whole.

The NAEP assessment in mathematics includes three types of questions:

- multiple choice
- short constructed-response
- extended constructed-response

What Is Adequate Yearly Progress (AYP)?

Under the provisions of the No Child Left Behind Act, states are required to document that all students are showing academic growth with respect to state standards. As some indicator of student progress, states are required to annually assess student performance in achieving specified objectives in mathematics. Houghton Mifflin Math *Adequate Yearly Progress Assessment Guide* provides many opportunities to monitor student progress over the course of the school year.

Copyright © Houghton Mifflin Company. All rights reserved.

Using Adequate Yearly Progress (AYP) Tests and Practice Tests

The Adequate Yearly Progress (AYP) Tests and Practice Tests in this book provide opportunities for assessing the content of Houghton Mifflin Math while offering test items that reflect the types of questions found in the NAEP tests.

Adequate Yearly Progress Tests

The No Child Left Behind Act has underscored the importance of ongoing and yearly testing. It requires that children's progress be measured and reported annually. The Adequate Yearly Progress Tests allow assessment of what students know and of how they think and reason mathematically. These assessments are designed to be used at the start of the school year, mid year, and again toward the end of the school year. The same concepts and skills are assessed in each test, allowing the teacher to monitor students' progress in building those mathematical skills and concepts that are core for that grade level. Further, the tests can assist the teacher in making decisions about how to improve learning throughout the year.

Practice Tests

The Practice Tests provide a thorough and balanced assessment of the content of each of the eight units in this grade level of Houghton Mifflin Math. Each Practice Test is designed to be used at the completion of the appropriate unit, but may be administered as a pretest to determine students' prior knowledge of the unit content.

Evaluating Student Performance

An Answer Key is provided in the back of this book for each Adequate Yearly Progress Test and Practice Test. Scoring Rubrics are found with the Answer Keys and are for use in evaluating short constructed-response and extended constructed-response questions. If you wish to score the Adequate Yearly Progress Tests, the point values shown on the next page may be used for the various types of questions. To obtain a percent score, multiply the Total Point Score by 2.

Copyright © Houghton Mifflin Company. All rights reserved.

As shown in the chart, two types of short constructed-response questions occur in the Adequate Yearly Progress Tests. Scoring rubrics give maximum values of 1 point or 2 points, depending on the complexity of the question. A 1-point scoring rubric is assigned to short constructed-response questions for which the student must supply a correct numerical or mathematical response. A 2-point scoring rubric is assigned to short constructed-response questions for which the student must supply a correct numerical or mathematical response and provide a brief explanation to support that response.

Scoring AYP Tests

Question Type and Distribution	Point Value	Total Points
Multiple Choice (32)	1	32
Short Constructed-Response (2)	1	2
Short Constructed-Response (4)	2	8
Extended Constructed-Response (2)	4	8

Extended constructed-response questions give a maximum value of 4 points. For these questions, the student is required to supply a correct numerical or mathematical response and a detailed explanation of how the result was arrived at, or the student must demonstrate the appropriate steps that were utilized to arrive at the solution.

The Practice Tests include the following distribution of questions.

Practice Tests Question Distribution

Grade	Multiple Choice	Short-Constructed Response	Extended-Constructed Response
3	18	1	1
4	16	2	2
5	16	2	2
6	16	2	2

If you wish to score the Practice Tests, the suggested point values are shown.

Scoring Practice Tests

Question Type	Student Point Score
Multiple Choice	1
Short-Constructed Response	2
Extended-Constructed Response	4

Use the conversion table to obtain a percent score.

Conversion Table

Grade	Student Point Score	Conversion Factor	Percent
3	x	4.2	y%
4–6	x	3.6	y%

Copyright © Houghton Mifflin Company. All rights reserved.

Test-Taking Tips

You may want to offer students the following advice for doing well on tests.

Strategies for Answering Multiple-Choice Questions

- Encourage students to read each question and all of the answer choices carefully, without skipping words or stopping at the first choice that appears to be correct.

- Point out the importance of looking at all the choices before choosing an answer. Explain that answers that are common mistakes are usually included in the choices.

- Emphasize that there is only one correct answer. Encourage educated guessing rather than leaving a question blank. Stress the value of recognizing incorrect choices and eliminating those from consideration. If unable to decide between two choices, encourage selection of their best guess.

- Caution students that on an actual standardized test, they should not make any extra marks near the answer bubbles as their answers might not be scored correctly.

- Before moving on to the next question, students should make sure their answer makes sense.

Strategies for Answering Constructed-Response Questions

- Tell students to read the problem once to be sure it makes sense to them. They should reread the problem to look for the information they need. Encourage them to try to picture the situation and predict what information is needed. In some cases making a drawing can help.

- Tell students to estimate whenever possible before solving a problem. They should use estimates to check that their answers are reasonable.

- Instruct students to write their answers on the write-on lines provided or make their drawings in the areas provided. When students are asked to show their work, space is usually provided below the question.

- If students can't give a complete answer, encourage them to show what they do know. Explain that they may receive some points for part of an answer.

Copyright © Houghton Mifflin Company. All rights reserved.

Before the Test Begins

- Preparation is the key to having students do well on any standardized tests. Explain the importance of preparing for tests by making sure to get enough sleep the night before the test and to eat a good breakfast that morning.

- First, remind students to read the directions carefully, and to make sure they understand what to do. If not, they should ask questions before beginning.

- Tell students not to spend too much time on one question. If a question seems difficult to answer, suggest they circle that question and go back to it later.

At the End of the Test

- Remind students to check their tests to make sure that every question has been answered and that one answer bubble has been filled in for each multiple-choice question.

Copyright © Houghton Mifflin Company. All rights reserved.

Houghton Mifflin
Math

Adequate Yearly Progress Tests

Fill in the letter of the correct answer.

1. What is the location of point Z?

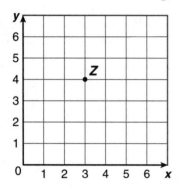

- **A** $(2, 3)$
- **B** $(3, 2)$
- **C** $(3, 4)$
- **D** $(4, 3)$

---

2. Brianne measured her rectangular-shaped bedroom. The perimeter was 42 feet. The width was 10 feet. If she uses x to represent the length, how can she represent the equation of the perimeter in a mathematical sentence?

- **A** $10x = 42$
- **B** $10 + x = 42$
- **C** $2(x + 10) = 42$
- **D** $x \div 10 = 42$

---

3. In the function, $y = 2x$, if x is replaced with 4, what does the function equal?

- **A** 64
- **B** 32
- **C** 16
- **D** 8

---

4. Anthony wrote and solved an equation in which the variable $x = 8$. Which of the following equations could be the equation Anthony wrote?

- **A** $x - 8 = 16$
- **B** $x + 8 = 16$
- **C** $2x = 4$
- **D** $2x = 8$

Copyright © Houghton Mifflin Company. All rights reserved.

Go On

5. What number belongs in the empty box, according to the patterns in the table?

2	4	8	16
6	12		48
18	36	72	144

(A) 18   (B) 24   (C) 30   (D) 336

---

6. Which pair of shapes below is congruent?

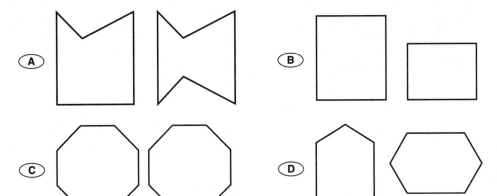

---

7. Which of the following choices shows the figure below after it has been flipped over the dotted line P?

(A)   (B)   (C)   (D)

Copyright © Houghton Mifflin Company. All rights reserved.

Go On

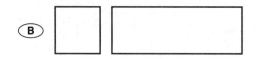

8. Which shapes below are similar?

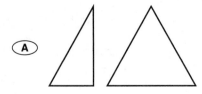

Ⓐ

Ⓑ

Ⓒ

Ⓓ

9. What type of angle is formed by the hands of the clock shown below?

Ⓐ right   Ⓑ obtuse   Ⓒ acute   Ⓓ straight

10. Mr. Thomas rides the commuter train between home and work five days a week. The ride takes 55 minutes one way. About how many hours does Mr. Thomas ride the train each week?

Ⓐ 2 hours   Ⓑ 5 hours   Ⓒ 10 hours   Ⓓ 20 hours

11. What animal weighs the closest to the weight of a mini-van?

Ⓐ cat   Ⓑ goat   Ⓒ pig   Ⓓ rhinoceros

Copyright © Houghton Mifflin Company. All rights reserved.

Go On

12. Alice measured her needle to the nearest $\frac{1}{2}$ inch. What is the length of the needle?

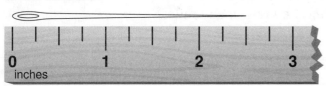

   Ⓐ $1\frac{1}{2}$ in.   Ⓑ 2 in.   Ⓒ $2\frac{1}{2}$ in.   Ⓓ 3 in.

---

13. Which unit is **best** for measuring the length of time it takes to drive 250 miles in a car?

   Ⓐ seconds   Ⓑ minutes   Ⓒ hours   Ⓓ days

---

14. Solve the following problem using order of operations.

$$9 \times (12 + 3)$$

   Ⓐ 39   Ⓑ 111   Ⓒ 135   Ⓓ 150

---

15. Rachel took a survey of 70 people, asking them to name their favorite school sports. When they answered, the participants were able to choose more than one sport. The results are shown below.

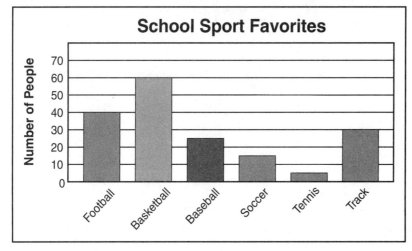

What percent of people likes track?

   Ⓐ 21%   Ⓑ 36%   Ⓒ 43%   Ⓓ 57%

Copyright © Houghton Mifflin Company. All rights reserved.

Go On

16. Lamont walked 1.745 miles to the store. He then walked 0.96 mile to his friend's house. Finally, he walked 0.352 mile back to his house. Round each distance to the nearest tenth and find how many miles Lamont walked altogether.

(A) 2.9 miles   (B) 3.0 miles   (C) 3.1 miles   (D) 3.2 miles

17. Which phrase is equal to 0.75?

(A) seventy-five   (B) seventy-five hundredths

(C) seventy-five thousandths   (D) seven and five hundredths

18. If $\frac{1}{5}$ of the pie was eaten, what percent of the pie is still left?

(A) 15%   (B) 20%   (C) 80%   (D) 85%

Use the information below to answer Questions 19 and 20.

Mr. Sullivan bought a rake for $5.31 and a water hose for $3.50. The prices included tax.

19. What was the total amount Mr. Sullivan spent?

(A) $5.66   (B) $8.53   (C) $8.81   (D) $5.67

Copyright © Houghton Mifflin Company. All rights reserved.

Go On

20. How much change will Mr. Sullivan receive from a $10 bill?

(A) $1.19   (B) $1.29   (C) $2.19   (D) $2.29

Use the information below to answer Questions 21, 22, and 23.

Mrs. Jones needs 18 squares of fabric to make a quilt. She chose $\frac{1}{3}$ red squares, $\frac{2}{9}$ blue squares, and $\frac{4}{9}$ white squares.

21. What fraction of total squares is blue or white?

(A) one-third   (B) one-half   (C) three-fourths   (D) two-thirds

---

22. If Mrs. Jones decides to make her quilt all red, how many more red squares will she need?

(A) 3   (B) 6   (C) 12   (D) 15

---

23. If Mrs. Jones decides to double the number of blue squares in the quilt without changing the total number of squares, what fraction of squares will be blue?

(A) $\frac{4}{18}$ (B) $\frac{2}{18}$ (C) $\frac{1}{9}$ (D) $\frac{4}{9}$

Copyright © Houghton Mifflin Company. All rights reserved.

Go On

24. Which is the greatest number of books that can be purchased with $10?

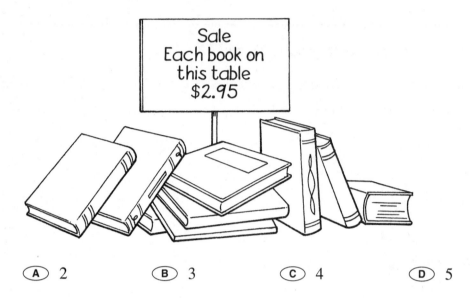

Sale
Each book on
this table
$2.95

(A) 2   (B) 3   (C) 4   (D) 5

---

25. In the first hour a newsstand was open, people bought 40 newspapers and 6 magazines. The newspapers sold for $0.35 each and the magazines for $2.95 each. How much did the newsstand make in that first hour?

(A) $15.85   (B) $19.75   (C) $26.50   (D) $31.70

---

26. What is the **best** method to solve the problem below?

Timmy needs bait, fishing line, and bobbers to go fishing. Bait costs $3.95, fishing line costs $1.25, and bobbers are $2.49. Can Timmy make his purchase with a $10 bill?

(A) mental computation   (B) paper and pencil

(C) calculator   (D) estimation

Copyright © Houghton Mifflin Company. All rights reserved.

Go On

27. Gerald weeded his mother's garden. He earned 10¢ for every weed he pulled. How much did he earn? What information is missing?

   (A) how many hours he worked   (B) how many weeds he pulled

   (C) how big the garden is   (D) how much money he had

28. In a board game, Jamie has many choices. Two pieces can be moved in three directions each, or two other pieces each have two choices. If Jamie must move one piece, how many options does she have?

   (A) 4   (B) 6   (C) 10   (D) 12

Use the information below to answer Questions 29, 30, and 31.

The following are the heights of middle-school students in Room 132.

3 ft 4 in.	4 ft 1 in.	3 ft 8 in.
4 ft 0 in.	4 ft 1 in.	4 ft 7 in.
4 ft 5 in.	4 ft 1 in.	4 ft 5 in.
5 ft 0 in.	5 ft 3 in.	4 ft 5 in.
3 ft 7 in.	4 ft 9 in.	3 ft 8 in.
4 ft 1 in.	3 ft 9 in.	4 ft 2 in.

29. What is the average of the height of the shortest student and the height of the tallest student?

   (A) higher than the median   (B) lower than the median

   (C) the same as the mode   (D) the same as the median

30. What is the mode of heights in Room 132?

   (A) 3 ft 8 in.   (B) 4 ft 1 in.   (C) 4 ft 5 in.   (D) 5 ft 3 in.

31. What is the range of heights?

   (A) 5 in.   (B) 1 ft 4 in.   (C) 2 ft 3 in.   (D) 1 ft 11 in.

Copyright © Houghton Mifflin Company. All rights reserved.

Go On

32. What is the probability of selecting a cube from the group of shapes?

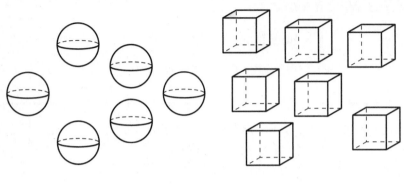

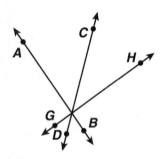

(A) $\frac{7}{6}$ (B) $\frac{7}{13}$ (C) $\frac{6}{7}$ (D) $\frac{6}{13}$

---

33. Which lines are perpendicular?

Answer: _____

---

34. What is the perimeter of a triangle with each side measuring
9 centimeters?

Answer: _____

---

35. The letters of the word "PROBABILITIES" were each on a separate
tile face down. If you picked one tile, which letter would you
most likely pick? Explain. Which letter would you be least likely
to pick? Explain.

Answer: _____

_____

_____

Copyright © Houghton Mifflin Company. All rights reserved.

Go On

36. What would be another pair of numbers that are related to each other in the way these pairs are? Fill in the table below.

First Number	6	8	9	
Second Number	3	5	6	

What is the relation of the second number to the first number in each pair?

Answer: _____

37. Look at the figures in the YES row and those in the NO row. Describe, in terms of geometry, one reason why the figures are grouped this way.

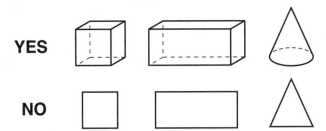

Answer: _____

_____

38. According to the graph below, which month(s) had twice as many days of rain as June?

Which months had the identical amounts of rainfall?

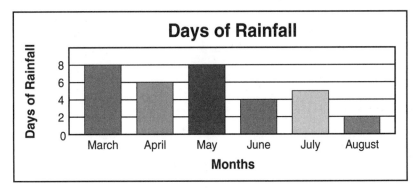

Answer: _____

_____

Copyright © Houghton Mifflin Company. All rights reserved.

Go On

39. Sean is ice-skating on a circular rink. If he skates along the outer part of the rink, how many degrees is it from the starting point all the way around the circle? If the rink has a radius of 24 feet, what is its diameter? What would be the circumference of this rink, using 3.14 for π?

Answer: _____

_____

_____

_____

40. If Sally works 72 hours at $5.00 an hour, and Tom works 84 hours at $4.00 an hour, how much do they earn together? Explain how you arrived at your answer.

Answer: _____

_____

_____

Copyright © Houghton Mifflin Company. All rights reserved.

Stop

Fill in the letter of the correct answer.

1. Which point has coordinates (3, 6)?

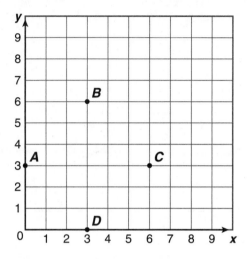

    Ⓐ A   Ⓑ B   Ⓒ C   Ⓓ D

2. David's age is 4 less than twice Jason's age. Which of the following expressions best represents David's age in relation to Jason's age?

    Ⓐ $2n - 4$ Ⓑ $4 - 2n$ Ⓒ $4n - 2$ Ⓓ $2 - 4n$

3. In the equation $y = 3x - 5$, if $x = 6$, what is the value of y?

    Ⓐ 4   Ⓑ 13   Ⓒ 31   Ⓓ 33

4. In the equation $n - 6 = 14$, what value can replace n?

    Ⓐ 8   Ⓑ 20   Ⓒ 22   Ⓓ 28

5. Which pair continues the pattern?

3	4	7	8	11	12	
10	11	14	15	18	19	

    Ⓐ 13, 21   Ⓑ 14, 21   Ⓒ 15, 22   Ⓓ 16, 22

Copyright © Houghton Mifflin Company. All rights reserved.

Go On ▶

6. Which figure below is congruent to the triangle in the box?

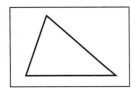

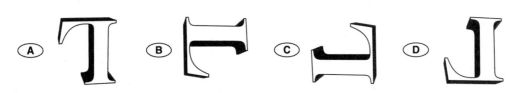

Ⓐ   Ⓑ   Ⓒ   Ⓓ

7. Which of the following is a reflection of this letter L?

Ⓐ   Ⓑ   Ⓒ   Ⓓ

8. Which pair of figures is similar?

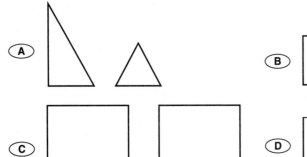

Ⓐ

Ⓑ

Ⓒ

Ⓓ

Copyright © Houghton Mifflin Company. All rights reserved.

Go On

9. Which figures have at least 2 right angles?

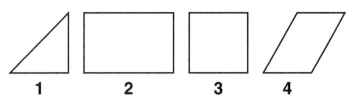

1   **2**   **3**   **4**

(A) 1 and 2   (B) 2 and 3   (C) 1 and 4   (D) 1 and 3

10. Which would be the best unit of measurement to describe how long it takes for a tree to grow several feet taller?

(A) week   (B) day   (C) year   (D) month

11. About how much does the watermelon below weigh?

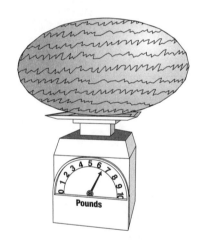

(A) 8 oz   (B) 14 oz   (C) 6 lbs, 8 oz   (D) 8 lbs

12. A student measures a pencil as shown below. What is the length of the pencil?

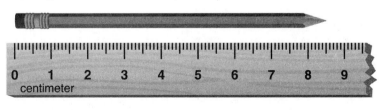

(A) 7.5 cm   (B) 8 cm   (C) 8.5 cm   (D) 9 cm

Copyright © Houghton Mifflin Company. All rights reserved.

Go On

13. Which would be the best unit of measurement for measuring the height of a small dog?

(A) millimeter   (B) centimeter   (C) meter   (D) kilometer

---

14. Solve the following problem using order of operations.

$$6 + 3 \times (1 + 7)$$

(A) 72   (B) 60   (C) 30   (D) 16

---

15. Rachel and Jerry went on a trip. The drive from their house to the airport took 28 minutes. Their flight was 2 hours, 25 minutes long. The drive to the hotel was 1 hour, 52 minutes long. About how long did the entire trip take from the house to the hotel?

(A) 3 hours   (B) 4 hours   (C) 5 hours   (D) 6 hours

---

16. What fraction of the students painted?

Thirty Students' Park Jobs

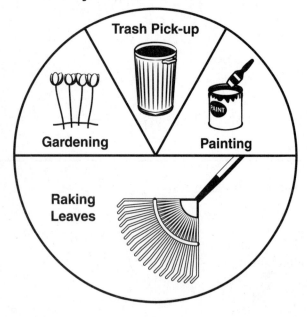

(A) $\frac{1}{4}$ (B) $\frac{1}{3}$ (C) $\frac{1}{2}$ (D) $\frac{1}{6}$

Copyright © Houghton Mifflin Company. All rights reserved.

Go On

17. Which decimal has the same value as $\frac{3}{10}$?

   A 0.3   **B** 0.03   **C** 3.0   **D** 0.003

18. Which number belongs in place of the question mark below?

$$\frac{1}{2} = \frac{?}{6}$$

   A 1   **B** 2   **C** 3   **D** 6

Use the information below to answer Questions 19 and 20.

Appliance	Power Used in Kilowatts
Radio	0.1
Television	0.23
Refrigerator	0.25
Clothes Dryer	4.2
Air Conditioner	1.28

19. What is the total power used by all of the household appliances listed in the chart?

   A 2.19 kilowatts   **B** 2.28 kilowatts

   C 6.06 kilowatts   **D** 6.56 kilowatts

20. If the dryer use were cut in half, what would be the total energy used by all of the appliances?

   A 1.86 kilowatts   **B** 2.19 kilowatts

   C 3.96 kilowatts   **D** 5.85 kilowatts

Copyright © Houghton Mifflin Company. All rights reserved.

Go On

Use the information below to answer Questions 21 and 22.

Tony has twice as many comic books as Rosa. Rosa has $\frac{2}{5}$ the number of comic books that Michael has. Michael has 15 comic books.

21. What fraction of the total comic books do Tony and Rosa own?

Ⓐ $\frac{18}{15}$ Ⓑ $\frac{6}{21}$ Ⓒ $\frac{18}{33}$ Ⓓ $\frac{21}{33}$

---

22. How many comic books does Tony have?

Ⓐ 6   Ⓑ 12   Ⓒ 21   Ⓓ 30

---

23. Apples are on sale for $0.29 a pound. To the nearest tenth, how many pounds can you get for $2.00?

Ⓐ 6.7 lbs   Ⓑ 6.9 lbs   Ⓒ 7.1 lbs   Ⓓ 7.3 lbs

Copyright © Houghton Mifflin Company. All rights reserved.

Go On ▶

24. Champion Sports was selling basketball shoes for $79.95. How much will 5 pairs of basketball shoes cost before sales tax is added?

 (A) $409.65   (B) $400.00

 (C) $399.75   (D) $355.55

25. A fast food restaurant sells 2 different size burgers. One has $\frac{1}{4}$ lb of meat. The other size has $\frac{1}{3}$ lb of meat. What is the difference in size?

 (A) $\frac{1}{3}$ lb   (B) $\frac{1}{4}$ lb

 (C) $\frac{1}{7}$ lb   (D) $\frac{1}{12}$ lb

26. Which of these problems would be **best** solved using mental math?

 (A) $3{,}245 \div 80$ (B) $3{,}245 \div 8$

 (C) $3{,}200 \div 80$ (D) $3{,}200 \div 88$

27. Jerry bought five cases of oil. He wants to know how many cans of oil he bought. What other information is needed?

 (A) where the oil was purchased

 (B) how many cans of oil were in each case

 (C) how many cans of oil were needed

 (D) how many trips were made to the store

28. How many different ways can you arrange the letters in MOM?

 (A) 1   (B) 2

 (C) 3   (D) 4

Copyright © Houghton Mifflin Company. All rights reserved.

Go On

Use the information in the table to answer Questions 29, 30, and 31.

Ten students spent some time practicing for an upcoming band concert. The following table shows the number of minutes each of the 5th grade band members spent in daily practice.

Student	Daily Practice (in minutes)	Instrument Played
Lisa	65	Violin
Juan	90	Bass
Marguerite	50	Trumpet
Peter	45	Bass
Magdalena	75	Violin
Jim	55	Clarinet
Alfonzo	80	Drums
Elena	50	Trumpet
Susan	60	Clarinet
Armando	30	Violin

29. What was the average number of minutes practiced by a student who plays the violin?

Ⓐ 56.6 minutes Ⓑ 70 minutes Ⓒ 85 minutes Ⓓ 170 minutes

30. All ten students practiced hard to prepare for the concert. For all the practice times listed below, which practice time appeared the most?

Ⓐ 45 minutes Ⓑ 50 minutes Ⓒ 55 minutes Ⓓ 90 minutes

31. Different students felt that they needed different amounts of practice time to prepare for the concert. What is the range in practice times?

Ⓐ 55 minutes Ⓑ 57 minutes Ⓒ 60 minutes Ⓓ 90 minutes

32. Salina had 4 red balloons and 6 blue balloons. Which ratio represents the probability of choosing a red balloon from the group?

Ⓐ $\frac{4}{6}$ Ⓑ $\frac{4}{10}$ Ⓒ $\frac{1}{4}$ Ⓓ $\frac{6}{10}$

Copyright © Houghton Mifflin Company. All rights reserved.

Go On▶

33. This chair has many line segments in it such as $\overline{AB}$, $\overline{HJ}$, and $\overline{IM}$. Name 2 pairs of line segments that are parallel and 2 pairs that are perpendicular. Assume that the chair is made with the seat parallel to the floor.

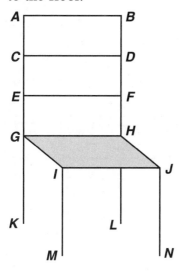

Answer: _____

_____

34. Find the perimeter of a rectangle 6 inches wide and 4 inches long.

Answer: _____

_____

35. On which color is the spinner most likely to land? Why?

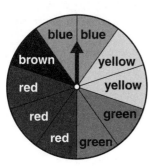

Answer: _____

_____

_____

Copyright © Houghton Mifflin Company. All rights reserved.

Go On

36. Look at this pattern of ordered pairs.

(1, 7), (3, 21), (5, 35), (☐, ☐)

What is the next ordered pair in the pattern? Explain how you found each number.

Answer: _____

_____

37. Describe three ways to sort the following shapes.

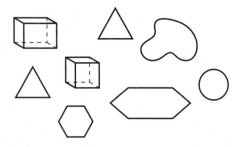

Answer: _____

_____

38. Look at the pictograph. How many votes did channel 10 receive?
Show your work or explain your answer.

Favorite TV Channel	
Channel	**Number of Votes**
2	📺 📺 📺
5	📺 📺 📺 📺 📺 📺
10	📺 📺
13	📺 📺 📺 📺
	📺 = 10 Votes

Answer: _____

_____

Copyright © Houghton Mifflin Company. All rights reserved.

Go On

39. Kevin put his dog, Bo, on a chain staked to the ground in the center of a circle. Bo was able to run around as far as the leash allowed him.

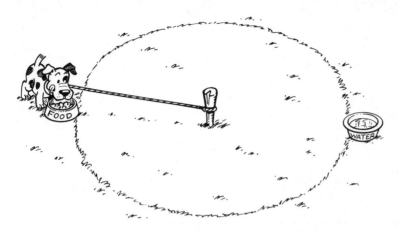

How many degrees around the circle did Bo move if he ran from his food bowl to his water dish? If the distance from the post to Bo's collar is 10 feet, what is the diameter of the circle? What is the circumference of the circle that Bo can run?

Answer: _____

_____

_____

_____

_____

40. The store clerk was placing bags of rice on the shelves. She put the 20-pound bags on the first shelf, the 10-pound bags on the second shelf, the 5-pound bags on the third shelf, and the 1-pound bags on the fourth shelf. When she was done, there were 7 bags of rice on the first shelf, 10 bags of rice on the second shelf, 15 bags of rice on the third shelf, and 21 bags of rice on the fourth shelf. How many pounds of rice were there on all the shelves combined? Explain how you arrived at your answer.

Answer: _____

_____

_____

Copyright © Houghton Mifflin Company. All rights reserved.

Stop

Fill in the letter of the correct answer.

1. What is the ordered pair for point Q?

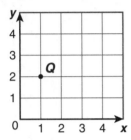

A (0, 2)   B (2, 0)   C (1, 2)   D (2, 1)

2. How can you algebraically represent 3 times Parker's age plus 6 if
   you use the letter p for Parker's age?

   A $3 + p \cdot 6$ B $3 \cdot 6 + p$ C $3 \cdot p + 6$ D $6 \cdot p + 3$

3. In the equation $y = 3x - 6$, what is the value of y if x equals 15?

   A 12   B 33   C 39   D 51

4. Which equation is true when $x = 5$?

   A $x + 9 = 16$ B $x - 8 = 13$ C $3x = 10$ D $x \div 5 = 1$

5. What is the rule for the number pattern in each row?

6	10
15	25
21	35
27	45
33	55

   A subtract 1, multiply by 2   B subtract 2, multiply by 2
   C divide by 3, multiply by 2   D divide by 3, multiply by 5

Copyright © Houghton Mifflin Company. All rights reserved.

Go On

6. Which figure below is congruent to the figure in the box?

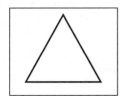

A   B   C   D

7. Which shows the letter after it is rotated a half turn?

A   B   C   D

8. Choose the triangle that is similar to figure 1.

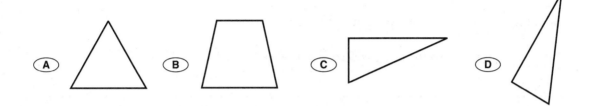

Figure 1

A   B C D

Copyright © Houghton Mifflin Company. All rights reserved.

Go On

9. Which of the following shapes has right angles?

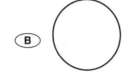 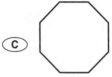  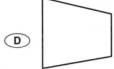

(A) (B) (C) (D)

10. About how long does it take to play a game of baseball?

(A) 3 days   (B) 3 hours   (C) 3 seconds   (D) 3 minutes

11. Which weighs about one gram?

(A) plum   (B) apple   (C) raisin   (D) watermelon

12. A student measures a pencil as shown below. What is the length of the pencil?

(A) 6 cm   (B) 6.5 cm   (C) 7 cm   (D) 7.5 cm

13. Which object below is used to measure temperature?

(A)

(B)

(C)

(D)

Copyright © Houghton Mifflin Company. All rights reserved.

Go On

14. Evaluate the expression using order of operations.

$$8 \times 9 - 4 \times 12$$

- (A) 24
- (B) 30
- (C) 48
- (D) 81

15. Which is the best estimate of $9{,}765 + 3{,}456$?

- (A) 9,000
- (B) 11,000
- (C) 13,000
- (D) 15,000

16. Which fraction is the same as 0.75?

- (A) $\frac{1}{4}$
- (B) $\frac{2}{4}$
- (C) $\frac{3}{4}$
- (D) $\frac{4}{4}$

17. The car company is offering a 0.09% interest rate. What is 0.09% in decimal form?

- (A) 0.9
- (B) 0.09
- (C) 0.009
- (D) 0.0009

18. Longville Middle School is hosting an extracurricular talent show. Ten out of 30 students in Mr. Martin's class are juggling in the talent show. In Mrs. O'Brien's class, nine out of 24 students are doing a skit. Eight out of 28 students in Mr. Hattori's class are singing a song. In Mrs. Ortiz's class, nine out of 27 students will do a dance number.

Which two teachers have the same fraction of their class participating in the talent show?

- (A) Mr. Martin and Mrs. Ortiz
- (B) Mr. Hattori and Mrs. Ortiz
- (C) Mr. Martin and Mrs. O'Brien
- (D) Mrs. O'Brien and Mr. Hattori

Copyright © Houghton Mifflin Company. All rights reserved.

Go On

Use the table below to answer Questions 19, 20, and 21.

A family of four ate dinner at Mike's restaurant on Tuesday.
This is the breakdown of their bill before taxes:

Mom	$20.86
Dad	$20.42
William	$12.73
Kendra	$12.84

19. What was the total bill for the family before sales tax?

    Ⓐ $66.85　　　Ⓑ $66.75　　　Ⓒ $65.85　　　Ⓓ $65.75

20. If William pays for his meal and Kendra's meal, and Mom pays
for her meal and Dad's meal, how much more will Mom's bill be
compared to William's?

    Ⓐ $15.51　　　Ⓑ $15.71　　　Ⓒ $16.51　　　Ⓓ $16.71

21. If sales tax is 5%, how would you figure the amount of tax to add
to the bill?

    Ⓐ multiply bill by 0.5　　　　Ⓑ multiply bill by 5.0

    Ⓒ multiply bill by 0.05　　　　Ⓓ multiply bill by 0.005

22. A stool has legs $14\frac{3}{8}$ in. high. The thickness of the seat is $\frac{5}{8}$ in.
What is the distance from the ground to the top of the stool?

    Ⓐ 14 in.　　　Ⓑ $14\frac{2}{8}$ in.　　　Ⓒ $14\frac{3}{5}$ in.　　　Ⓓ 15 in.

Copyright © Houghton Mifflin Company. All rights reserved.

Go On

23. If a pack of 13 candles costs $6.50, about how much does each candle cost?

(A) $0.25

(B) $0.50

(C) $0.75

(D) $1.00

24. Nicole found a can of paint $\frac{2}{3}$ full. She used $\frac{3}{4}$ of what was left to paint her bedroom. How much of the whole can of paint did she use?

(A) $\frac{1}{12}$ of the can

(B) $\frac{17}{12}$ of the can

(C) $\frac{1}{2}$ of the can

(D) $\frac{1}{4}$ of the can

25. A $1\frac{1}{2}$ foot log was cut from a fallen $16\frac{1}{2}$ foot tree. How long is the remaining tree?

(A) 18 feet

(B) 16 feet

(C) $15\frac{1}{2}$ feet

(D) 15 feet

26. Which should Paulo think about to make it easier to multiply 37×99 in his head?

(A) 99 as $100 - 1$

(B) 37 as $35 + 2$

(C) 99 as $90 + 9$

(D) 37 as $30 + 7$

27. What information is needed to solve this problem?

Cindy has $6.45. If she buys a stuffed animal, how much money will she have left?

(A) the stuffed animal is a purple elephant

(B) how much Cindy's allowance was

(C) how much the stuffed animal costs

(D) how much change Cindy gets back

Copyright © Houghton Mifflin Company. All rights reserved.

Go On

28. Dinner consists of a combination of 1 meat, 1 vegetable, and 1 bread.

Meats: chicken, beef, or pork
Breads: rolls, potatoes, or rice
Vegetables: broccoli, cauliflower, carrots, or green beans

How many different dinners can be made?

(A) 7   (B) 10   (C) 18   (D) 36

Use the table below to answer Questions 29, 30, and 31.

The lengths of different clubs used at a local golf range are listed below.

Club Lengths in Inches		
32	31	32
30	34	35
31	32	36
37	35	32

29. What is the average length club that the golf range offers?

(A) 30-inch club   (B) 31-inch club
(C) 32-inch club   (D) 33-inch club

30. One club seems to be most popular at the golf range.
Which of the club lengths appears most often?

(A) 30-inch club   (B) 31-inch club
(C) 32-inch club   (D) 35-inch club

31. What is the range in club sizes that the golf facility offers its customers?

(A) 7   (B) 12
(C) 30   (D) 37

Copyright © Houghton Mifflin Company. All rights reserved.

Go On

32. Jason has 3 red T-shirts and 5 blue T-shirts. Which ratio represents the probability of choosing a red shirt from the group?

Ⓐ $\frac{3}{5}$ Ⓑ $\frac{3}{8}$ Ⓒ $\frac{8}{3}$ Ⓓ $\frac{8}{5}$

---

33. How would you describe the relationship between lines *EH* and *FG*?

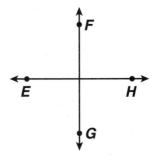

Answer: _____

---

34. Find the perimeter of this parallelogram.

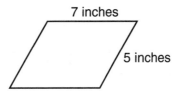

Answer: _____

---

35. If you shake the bag below to mix the numbers, which numbers are most likely to be pulled out and why?

Answer: _____

_____

_____

Copyright © Houghton Mifflin Company. All rights reserved.

36. Fill in the blank boxes with the next ordered pair of numbers needed to complete the chart. Then explain how you found your answer.

2	10
3	15
4	20

Answer: _____

_____

_____

37. Describe three differences between the two figures below.

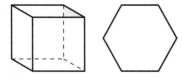

Answer: _____

_____

_____

_____

38. Ramona's team scored a total of 168 runs in four years. How many runs were scored in the fourth year?

Runs Scored	
1st year	⚾ ⚾ ⚾ ⚾
2nd year	⚾ ⚾
3rd year	⚾ ⚾ ⚾
4th year	
	⚾ = 12 Runs

Answer: _____

Copyright © Houghton Mifflin Company. All rights reserved.

Go On ▶

39. Mr. Molina traced a circle onto a sheet of paper. He then drew some line segments and labeled the end points.

Mr. Molina had his class measure the diameter of the circle and found that it was 4 centimeters long. What is the length of the radius?

How many degrees were between point *C* and point *D*? What is the circumference of the circle using 3.14 for π ?

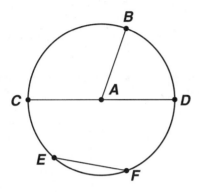

Answer: _____

_____

_____

_____

_____

40. Tom rode his bicycle to the store from his house. He rode at 12 mph for 15 minutes. How many miles did Tom ride from his house to the store and back? Explain how you solved this problem.

Answer: _____

_____

_____

_____

Copyright © Houghton Mifflin Company. All rights reserved.

Stop

Practice
Tests

Name _____ Date _____

Fill in the letter of the correct answer.

1. Which is the standard form of this number?

900,000 + 40,000 + 200 + 10 + 3

- (A) 940,200,013
- (B) 900,421,003
- (C) 900,420,103
- (D) 940,213

---

2. Which group of numbers is ordered from greatest to least?

- (A) 489.3; 48.92; 4.894
- (B) 4.894; 48.92; 489.3
- (C) 4.894; 489.3; 48.92
- (D) 48.92; 489.3; 4.894

---

3. Which equation is true if $n = 3$?

- (A) $47 + n = 50$
- (B) $47 = n + 50$
- (C) $47 - n = 50$
- (D) $n - 50 = 47$

---

4. Which group of items costs the most? Estimate to find the answer.

- (A) 2 large avocados
- (B) 3 grapefruits
- (C) 4 pounds of onions
- (D) 5 small avocados

---

5. Jean Lafitte National Park in Louisiana is 20,020 acres. New Bedford Whaling National Park in Massachusetts is 34 acres. What is the difference in their sizes?

- (A) 20,054 acres
- (B) 20,014 acres
- (C) 19,986 acres
- (D) 19,096 acres

Copyright © Houghton Mifflin Company. All rights reserved.

Go On

6. What is the value of *n* in this equation?

$n + n = 48$

Ⓐ 96　　　Ⓑ 48　　　Ⓒ 36　　　Ⓓ 24

---

7. How would you write this decimal in words?

40.326

Ⓐ forty thousandths, three hundred twenty-six

Ⓑ forty and three hundred twenty-six thousandths

Ⓒ forty thousand, three hundred twenty-six hundredths

Ⓓ forty point three two six

---

8. If *n* = 12, what is the value of this expression?

$(28 + n) + (n + 13)$

Ⓐ 12　　　Ⓑ 25　　　Ⓒ 40　　　Ⓓ 65

---

9. What is the difference in the land areas of these two states?

KANSAS
81,823 square miles

ARKANSAS
52,075
square
miles

Ⓐ 29,748 square miles　　　Ⓑ 29,847 square miles

Ⓒ 31,852 square miles　　　Ⓓ 39,858 square miles

---

10. What is the value of *n* in this equation?

$n + 41 = 45$

Ⓐ 3　　　Ⓑ 4　　　Ⓒ 14　　　Ⓓ 86

Copyright © Houghton Mifflin Company. All rights reserved.

Go On ▶

11. What is the place value of the underlined digit?

372,4<u>6</u>1,589

- (A) six hundred thousand
- (B) sixty thousand
- (C) six hundred
- (D) sixty

12. What is the difference?

$$\begin{array}{r} 3{,}783{,}014 \\ -\ 1{,}792{,}586 \\ \hline \end{array}$$

- (A) 1,990,428
- (B) 1,991,538
- (C) 2,001,572
- (D) 5,575,600

13. What is the value of x in this equation?

$32 - x = 22$

- (A) 8
- (B) 10
- (C) 14
- (D) 54

14. Which statement is true?

- (A) 457 < 382
- (B) 382 > 457
- (C) 457 > 382
- (D) 382 = 457

15. On Saturday 679 people attended the art show. On Sunday 483 people attended. If each number is rounded to the nearest hundred, about how many people attended the art show in the two days?

- (A) 1,200
- (B) 1,160
- (C) 1,100
- (D) 1,000

16. Sam's savings account earned $298.4864 in interest. How much money is that, rounded to the nearest hundredth?

- (A) $300.00
- (B) $298.50
- (C) $298.49
- (D) $298.486

Copyright © Houghton Mifflin Company. All rights reserved.

Go On

17. Marvin walked across each of these bridges during his trip around the world.

Bridge	Location	Length of Main Span
Akashi Kaikyo	Hyogo, Japan	6,529 feet
Brooklyn Bridge	East River, New York City	1,596 feet
Golden Gate	San Francisco Bay, San Francisco	4,200 feet
First Bosporus	Istanbul, Turkey	3,524 feet

Which bridge is the second longest? How far did Marvin walk when he crossed that bridge?

Answer: _____

How much farther than that did Marvin walk when he crossed the longest bridge?

Answer: _____

18. Write and solve an equation in which you find the difference in the heights of these two buildings.

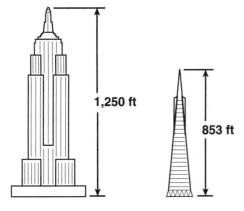

1,250 ft

853 ft

Answer: _____

_____

Copyright © Houghton Mifflin Company. All rights reserved.

Go On

19. The fifth-grade class at Jefferson Middle School has 23 students. The fifth-grade class at Madison Middle School has 5 more students than that. The fifth-grade class at Washington Middle School has 3 more students than Madison has. What is the total number of fifth-grade students at the three schools? Show your work, and explain each step.

Answer: _____

_____

_____

20. Darla bought a sweater. She gave the salesperson $40.00 and received $7.61 in change. Use an equation to find out how much Darla's sweater cost. Show all your work.

Answer: _____

_____

_____

Copyright © Houghton Mifflin Company. All rights reserved.

Stop

Fill in the letter of the correct answer.

1. The school cafeteria served 4 celery sticks to each of 48 students. How many celery sticks were served in all?

   Ⓐ 172   Ⓑ 184   Ⓒ 192   Ⓓ 202

2. Which multiplication expression represents the total number of squares in the rectangle?

   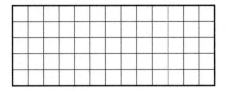

   Ⓐ (5 × 10) + (5 × 3)   Ⓑ (5 × 5) + (5 × 5)

   Ⓒ (5 × 5) + (3 × 10)   Ⓓ (5 × 12)

3. Last year 58 people bought teddy bears at the crafts fair. This year 4 times that number bought teddy bears. About how many people bought bears this year?

   Ⓐ 54   Ⓑ 62   Ⓒ 200   Ⓓ 240

4. What is the value of x?

   $42 \div x = 6$

   Ⓐ 7   Ⓑ 8   Ⓒ 36   Ⓓ 48

5. Ben spent $59.50 for lunches over a period of 14 days. About how much did he spend each day?

   Ⓐ $2.50   Ⓑ $4.00   Ⓒ $8.00   Ⓓ $14.00

Copyright © Houghton Mifflin Company. All rights reserved.

Go On

6. Which expression is **not** shown by the diagram?

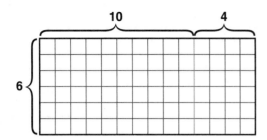

- Ⓐ 6 × 14
- Ⓑ (6 × 10) + (6 × 4)
- Ⓒ 6 (10 + 4)
- Ⓓ 10 (6 × 4)

---

7. What is the quotient?

938 ÷ 7

- Ⓐ 124
- Ⓑ 134
- Ⓒ 138
- Ⓓ 140

---

8. What is the value of *r*?

28 = 7*r*
r = ☐

- Ⓐ 35
- Ⓑ 21
- Ⓒ 4
- Ⓓ 3

---

9. What is the quotient?

962 ÷ 36

- Ⓐ 26 R26
- Ⓑ 26 R72
- Ⓒ 30
- Ⓓ 32 R18

---

10. Myra sold 48 used CDs. Which expression shows a quick way to estimate how much money Myra collected?

- Ⓐ $8.27 × 48
- Ⓑ $8 × 50
- Ⓒ $8 × 40
- Ⓓ $9 × 50

Copyright © Houghton Mifflin Company. All rights reserved.

Go On

11. Use mental math to find what n represents.

$3n = 45$

(A) 15   (B) 42   (C) 48   (D) 135

12. Which expression is a simplified version of this one?

$(8 \times 4) + 3^2 - (12 + 6)$

(A) $8 \times 12^2 - 18$ (B) $8 \times 4 - 3^2 - 12 + 6$

(C) $32 + 9 - 18$ (D) $(32) + (3^2 - 12 + 6)$

13. Which number sentence demonstrates the Distributive Property?

(A) $8 \times 14 = 112$ (B) $8 \times 14 = (8 \times 10) + (8 \times 4)$

(C) $8 \times 14 = 14 \times 8$ (D) $8 \times 14 = 2 \times 56$

14. What is the value of n?

$(36 \div 6) - (11 - 5) = n$
$n = \square$

(A) 0   (B) 4   (C) 5   (D) 6

15. The school's 86 computers have to be shared by 516 students. How many students must share each computer?

(A) 5   (B) 6   (C) 16   (D) 60

16. What is the value of n?

$(48 \div 6) - (2 \times 3) = n$
$n = \square$

(A) 8   (B) 6   (C) 4   (D) 2

Copyright © Houghton Mifflin Company. All rights reserved.

Go On

17. Justine is waiting in line for an amusement park ride. There are
155 people ahead of her. Each car on the ride holds 8 people.
How many cars will have to be filled before Justine gets a seat?
Show all your work and explain your answer.

Answer: _____

_____

_____

18. Maurice wants to buy a DVD player for $238. If he earns $6 an hour,
about how many hours will he have to work to pay for the DVD player?
Use mental math to estimate. Explain your answer.

Answer: _____

_____

19. Emma and Dave planted pansies in the flowerbeds. Emma planted
3 times as many as Dave. If Emma planted 45, how many did Dave
plant? How many pansies did they plant in all? Write an equation
to solve each part of the problem.

Answer: _____

_____

_____

20. Roberto has 126 CDs. He has 5 rock-and-roll CDs for every
4 jazz CDs. How many rock-and-roll CDs does Roberto have?
How many jazz CDs does he have? Explain your answer.

Answer: _____

_____

_____

Copyright © Houghton Mifflin Company. All rights reserved.

Stop

Fill in the letter of the correct answer.

Use the following data to answer Questions 1–2.

Hours Spent Doing Homework per Week							
11	10	2	9	4	5	7	8

1. What is the range of the data?

    A 2   **B** 5   **C** 9   **D** 11

2. What is the mean of the data?

    A 9   **B** 7   **C** 6   **D** 5

3. What would be a normal serving of juice for one person at breakfast?

    A 20 milliliters   **B** 200 milliliters

    C 750 milliliters   **D** 1 liter

4. How many more fifth-grade students ride the bus than walk to school?

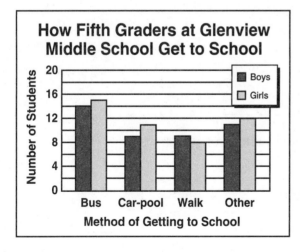

    A 12   **B** 15   **C** 17   **D** 29

Copyright © Houghton Mifflin Company. All rights reserved.

Go On

5. How long is the ribbon?

- (A) 4 inches
- (B) $4\frac{1}{2}$ inches
- (C) $4\frac{3}{4}$ inches
- (D) 5 inches

6. Which circle graph could be used to show the following data?

50% of fifth graders prefer dogs for pets
16% of fifth graders prefer cats for pets
17% of fifth graders prefer birds for pets
17% of fifth graders prefer rabbits for pets

(A)   (B)

(C)   (D)

7. To prepare for the school picnic, students made 25 gallons of punch. How many quarts of punch did they make?

- (A) 250
- (B) 150
- (C) 100
- (D) 50

Copyright © Houghton Mifflin Company. All rights reserved.

Go On

8. What is the difference in the temperatures recorded on
Sunday and Friday?

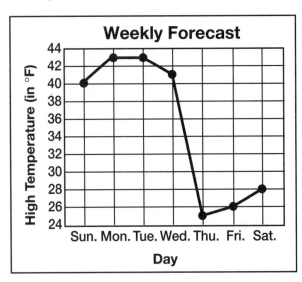

A. 14 degrees B. 26 degrees C. 40 degrees D. 66 degrees

9. Which bar graph displays the same information that
is in this tally chart?

Favorite Fruits	Tally	Total
banana	||||	4
orange	||	2
apple	|||	3
grapes	||	2

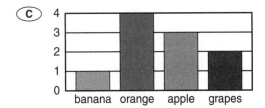
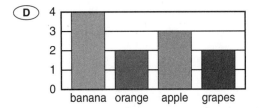

Copyright © Houghton Mifflin Company. All rights reserved.

Go On

Name _____   Date _____

10. Jane wants to make a graph that shows how her savings account grew each month for a year. Which kind of graph is her best choice?

(A) bar graph   (B) pictograph

(C) circle graph   (D) line graph

Use the line plot to answer Questions 11–12.

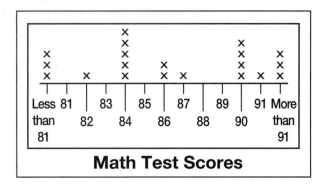

Math Test Scores

11. What is the median test score?

(A) 81   (B) 83   (C) 86   (D) 91

---

12. What is the mode of the data set?

(A) less than 81   (B) 84

(C) 90   (D) more than 91

---

13. Sam wants to make a graph to display and compare sales figures for two different products over a period of a year. Which type of graph would be best for Sam to use?

(A) circle graph   (B) line graph

(C) double line graph   (D) pictograph

Copyright © Houghton Mifflin Company. All rights reserved.

Go On

Use the table to answer Questions 14–16.

Average Life Spans of Animals	
Cat	12 years
Dog	12 years
Elephant	40 years
Gorilla	20 years
Horse	20 years
Lion	15 years
Rabbit	5 years

14. What is the difference between the shortest average life span and the longest?

   Ⓐ 24 years   Ⓑ 35 years   Ⓒ 40 years   Ⓓ 45 years

15. Which animals can be expected to live about 4 times as long as a rabbit?

   Ⓐ cat and dog   Ⓑ lion and horse

   Ⓒ elephant and gorilla   Ⓓ gorilla and horse

16. Dana wants to observe gorillas in the wild from birth to death. What is the minimum number of years she should plan to devote to this project?

   Ⓐ 5 years   Ⓑ 12 years   Ⓒ 20 years   Ⓓ 40 years

17. About 32,800 bottles of water are sold at a baseball game. Each bottle contains 16 fluid ounces. How many gallons is this?

Answer: _____

Copyright © Houghton Mifflin Company. All rights reserved.

Go On

18. Every day for the past week, Dennis has kept track of the price of a stock he owns. He made this graph to show how the price changed. Explain why Dennis's graph is misleading. Then, use the blank grid to make a new graph that better represents the stock's performance.

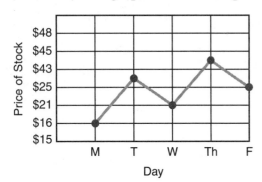

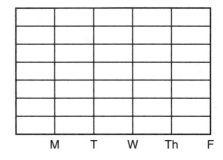

Answer: _____

_____

_____

19. Five students had their heights measured in inches. Their heights are shown in the table below. Complete the table by recording their heights in feet and inches. Then list the students in order from tallest to shortest.

Student	Height (in inches)	Height (in feet and inches)
Dena	59	
Albert	52	
Jacob	49	
Tiffany	47	
Lavonne	55	

Answer: _____

_____

Copyright © Houghton Mifflin Company. All rights reserved.

Go On

20. Fifth-grade girls in one class were asked how many stories they read in a week. These are the answers 11 girls gave: 3, 1, 3, 1, 1, 2, 3, 3, 1, 3, 2. Complete this bar graph to show their answers. Then answer the questions below.

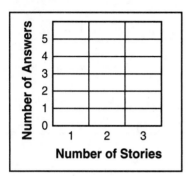

What is the mode of this data?

Answer: _____

What is the range?

Answer: _____

Copyright © Houghton Mifflin Company. All rights reserved.

Stop

Name _____ Date _____

Fill in the letter of the correct answer.

1. Which number is a prime number?

(A) 4   (B) 9   (C) 11   (D) 12

---

2. Which pair of fractions is equivalent?

(A) $\frac{2}{3}$ $\frac{3}{2}$ (B) $\frac{1}{2}$ $\frac{5}{12}$

(C) $\frac{7}{8}$ $\frac{49}{58}$ (D) $\frac{2}{3}$ $\frac{12}{18}$

---

3. Dora has 45 red beads and 60 green beads. What is the greatest number of pins she can make if she must use all the beads and if each pin must look exactly alike?

(A) 15   (B) 30   (C) 60   (D) 105

---

4. Mia saved $68.11 in May and $59.83 in June. About how much more did she save in May than in June? Estimate to find the answer.

(A) $8.00   (B) $8.28   (C) $9.00   (D) $128.00

---

5. What is the LCM of 18 and 27?

(A) 486   (B) 108   (C) 54   (D) 45

---

6. What factor completes this factor tree?

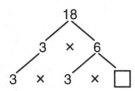

(A) 1   (B) 2   (C) 3   (D) 12

Copyright © Houghton Mifflin Company. All rights reserved.

Go On

7. Gregory served 6 of these pieces of pie at a party. What fractional part of the pie did he serve? Choose the answer that shows the simplest form.

(A) $\frac{2}{8}$

(B) $\frac{1}{4}$

(C) $\frac{6}{8}$

(D) $\frac{3}{4}$

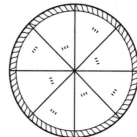

8. What mixed number does point A represent?

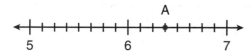

(A) $\frac{3}{8}$

(B) $6\frac{1}{4}$

(C) $6\frac{3}{8}$

(D) $6\frac{1}{2}$

9. What is the sum?

14.76
+ 33.85

(A) 20.91

(B) 40.81

(C) 47.51

(D) 48.61

10. Which mixed number is the equivalent of 3.8, expressed in its simplest form?

(A) $3\frac{1}{8}$

(B) $3\frac{80}{100}$

(C) $3\frac{8}{10}$

(D) $3\frac{4}{5}$

11. Jean walks her dog every day. On Monday they walked $3\frac{3}{4}$ miles. On Tuesday they walked $2\frac{1}{4}$ miles. On Wednesday they walked $2\frac{7}{8}$ miles. About how many miles did they walk on those three days? Estimate to find the answer.

(A) about 6 miles

(B) about 7 miles

(C) about 8 miles

(D) about 9 miles

Copyright © Houghton Mifflin Company. All rights reserved.

Go On

12. Which number is a common factor of both 24 and 30?

   (A) 5   (B) 6   (C) 8   (D) 12

13. What is the sum?

$$11\frac{1}{4}$$
$$+\ \ 4\frac{3}{8}$$

   (A) $15\frac{5}{8}$ (B) $15\frac{4}{12}$ (C) $7\frac{5}{8}$ (D) $6\frac{7}{8}$

14. Which list shows the numbers in order from greatest to least?

$$\frac{1}{3},\ 0.48,\ \frac{1}{9},\ 0.3$$

   (A) $0.48,\ \frac{1}{3},\ 0.3,\ \frac{1}{9}$ (B) $\frac{1}{9},\ 0.3,\ \frac{1}{3},\ 0.48$

   (C) $0.48,\ 0.3,\ \frac{1}{3},\ \frac{1}{9}$ (D) $0.3,\ \frac{1}{3},\ 0.48,\ \frac{1}{9}$

15. Gloria used $8\frac{3}{8}$ yards of fabric for her costume. Jim used $9\frac{3}{4}$ yards for his costume. How much more fabric did Jim use than Gloria?

   (A) $1\frac{1}{4}$ yards   (B) $1\frac{3}{8}$ yards

   (C) $1\frac{6}{12}$ yards   (D) $18\frac{1}{8}$ yards

16. What is the difference?

$$8.7825$$
$$-\ 2.5983$$

   (A) 6.1732   (B) 6.1842   (C) 6.2162   (D) 11.3808

Copyright © Houghton Mifflin Company. All rights reserved.

17. Find the difference.

$6\frac{3}{8} - 3\frac{5}{8}$

Write your answer in simplest form. Then explain each step in your solution.

Answer: _____

_____

18. Dan saved these amounts of money three months in a row: $76.81, $89.43, and $63.37. How much did he save in all?

Answer: _____

_____

If he adds this sum to his savings account of $832.79, what will his total be?

Answer: _____

_____

19. Michael has 56 pens and 72 toy cars. He wants to make up identical gift bags to give out at a party. Using all the items and putting the same items in each bag, what is the greatest number of gift bags Michael can make? What will be in each gift bag?

Answer: _____

_____

_____

Copyright © Houghton Mifflin Company. All rights reserved.

20. Ashby donated 3.7 pounds of aluminum cans to the fund-raising drive. Dale donated $8\frac{3}{4}$ pounds, Michelle donated 4.3 pounds, and Craig donated $7\frac{1}{4}$ pounds. How many pounds in all did the four students donate? Find the answer in mixed numbers and in decimal form. Show all your work.

Answer: _____

_____

_____

Copyright © Houghton Mifflin Company. All rights reserved.

Stop

Fill in the letter of the correct answer.

1. Of the 96 singers who tried out for the choir, $\frac{3}{8}$ were tenors. How many of them were tenors?

   (A) 8   (B) 12   (C) 36   (D) 40

---

2. Estimate the quotient.

   $24.89 \div 6.3$

   (A) 0.04   (B) 4   (C) 40   (D) 150

---

3. Which of the following does NOT have a product of 0.00036?

   (A) 0.009×0.04 (B) 0.12×0.003 (C) 0.018×0.02 (D) 0.06×0.06

---

4. What is the quotient?

   $19\frac{1}{2} \div 4\frac{7}{8}$

   (A) $3\frac{3}{4}$ (B) 4   (C) $7\frac{3}{4}$ (D) 9

---

5. Which estimate makes the most sense?

   8.89×0.3

   (A) 0.27   (B) 3   (C) 24   (D) 270

---

6. Bob filled his gas tank with 16.5 gallons of gas. He drove 445.5 miles on that tank. About how many miles per gallon (mi/gal) did he get?

   (A) 3 mi/gal   (B) 15 mi/gal   (C) 30 mi/gal   (D) 50 mi/gal

---

7. Josie practices soccer $7\frac{1}{2}$ hours each week. She practices for $1\frac{1}{4}$ hours each day. How many days per week does she practice?

   (A) 3 days   (B) 4 days   (C) 5 days   (D) 6 days

Copyright © Houghton Mifflin Company. All rights reserved.

Go On

8. Here is a list of ingredients for a recipe based on carrots. It serves 8. Manny wants to make the recipe for 4 people. How many cups of carrots will he need?

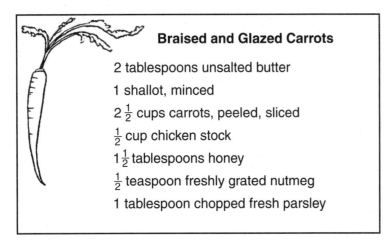

Braised and Glazed Carrots

2 tablespoons unsalted butter

1 shallot, minced

$2\frac{1}{2}$ cups carrots, peeled, sliced

$\frac{1}{2}$ cup chicken stock

$1\frac{1}{2}$ tablespoons honey

$\frac{1}{2}$ teaspoon freshly grated nutmeg

1 tablespoon chopped fresh parsley

(A) $1\frac{1}{4}$ cups   (B) $2\frac{1}{2}$ cups   (C) 4 cups   (D) 5 cups

9. Which describes the relationship between these quotients?

$54.3 \div 3 \square 98.4 \div 6$

(A) $54.3 \div 3 = 98.4 \div 6$ (B) $54.3 \div 3 < 98.4 \div 6$

(C) $54.3 \div 3 > 98.4 \div 6$ (D) $98.4 \div 6 > 54.3 \div 3$

10. What is the product?

8.29×3.43

(A) 2843.47   (B) 284.347   (C) 28.4347   (D) 2.84347

11. What is the area of Donna's Persian carpet?

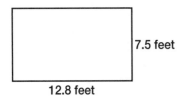

7.5 feet

12.8 feet

(A) 33.1 square feet   (B) 40.6 square feet

(C) 79.6 square feet   (D) 96 square feet

Copyright © Houghton Mifflin Company. All rights reserved.

Go On

12. Dan kept track on a calendar of distances he ran. Here is his record for the first two weeks of January. About how many miles did he run?

January						
Sun	**Mon**	**Tues**	**Wed**	**Thurs**	**Fri**	**Sat**
	9.5 miles		9.5 miles		9.5 miles	9.5 miles
	9.5 miles	9.5 miles		9.5 miles		9.5 miles

Ⓐ 7.6   Ⓑ 28   Ⓒ 80   Ⓓ 360

13. Kareem bought 4.5 pounds of sliced turkey. If the turkey cost $3.26 per pound, how much did Kareem spend on it?

Ⓐ $29.34   Ⓑ $14.67   Ⓒ $14.57   Ⓓ $13.37

14. What is the product?

$5\frac{3}{5} \times 2\frac{1}{2}$

Ⓐ $2\frac{6}{25}$ Ⓑ 7   Ⓒ $7\frac{3}{10}$ Ⓓ 14

15. What is the quotient?

96.5 ÷ 8

Ⓐ 1.20625   Ⓑ 12.0625   Ⓒ 120.625   Ⓓ 772

16. Estimate.

0.96 × 0.4

Ⓐ 36   Ⓑ 2.5   Ⓒ 3.8   Ⓓ 0.4

Copyright © Houghton Mifflin Company. All rights reserved.

Go On

17. On Saturday, 0.35 of the invited guests showed up for a party. If 60 people had been invited, how many failed to show up? Show your work in the space below.

Answer: _____

_____

18. A recipe calls for $1\frac{1}{4}$ cups of sugar. Don wants to triple the recipe so he can serve 12 people. If each portion has the same amount of sugar, how much sugar is in each person's serving? Show your work in the space below.

Answer: _____

_____

19. Jan walked $23\frac{2}{5}$ miles in 9 hours. Basil walked $12\frac{3}{4}$ miles in $4\frac{1}{4}$ hours. Whose average walking speed is faster? Show your work, and explain your answer.

Answer: _____

_____

_____

20. Katie worked 26 hours and earned $292.50. Brett worked 33 hours and earned $354.75. Whose hourly wage is greater? How much greater is it? Show all your work below.

Answer: _____

_____

Copyright © Houghton Mifflin Company. All rights reserved.

Stop

Fill in the letter of the correct answer.

1. Manuel wants to put a border around his flower garden. How many feet of border material will he need?

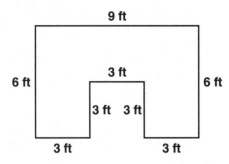

   9 ft

6 ft   3 ft   6 ft

   3 ft 3 ft

  3 ft   3 ft

Ⓐ 36 feet   Ⓑ 30 feet   Ⓒ 27 feet   Ⓓ 18 feet

2. What is the name of this figure?

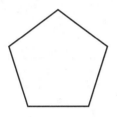

Ⓐ quadrilateral   Ⓑ trapezoid

Ⓒ octagon   Ⓓ pentagon

3. Which figures are congruent?

Ⓐ 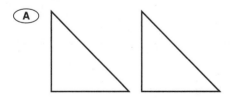   Ⓑ

Ⓒ 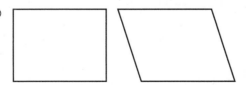   Ⓓ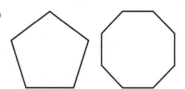

Copyright © Houghton Mifflin Company. All rights reserved.

Go On ▶

4. What is the circumference of a circle that has a diameter of
19 mm? (Use 3.14 for π).

(A) 59.66 mm   (B) 59.36 mm

(C) 31.4 mm   (D) 22.14 mm

5. Which figure does not have rotational symmetry?

(A)

(B)

(C)

(D)

6. Dylan is using plastic letters to make a sign. He needs one
more lowercase "d" to complete the sign. What is one option?

(A) He could use the letter "p" and change it by a reflection across
a horizontal line.

(B) He could use the letter "b" and change it by a reflection across
a vertical line.

(C) He could use the letter "p" and change it by a translation.

(D) He could use the letter "b" and rotate it 180°.

7. Mia is decorating round ornaments. Each ornament has a diameter
of 3 inches. If she puts ribbon around the circumference of each
ornament, how much ribbon will she need to decorate 10 ornaments?
(Use 3.14 for π).

(A) 9.32 inches   (B) 30 inches

(C) 9.42 inches   (D) 94.2 inches

Copyright © Houghton Mifflin Company. All rights reserved.

Go On ▶

8. Delbert rotated the following shape 360°. What was the final result?

A

B

C

D

---

9. Miriam wants to add wall-to-wall carpet to this room. What is the area that she will have to cover?

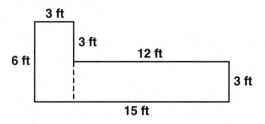

A   81 square feet   B   54 square feet

C   42 square feet   D   36 square feet

---

10. Darlene is making a fabric-covered stand for a sculpture. How much fabric will she need to cover this rectangular prism?

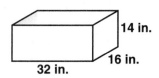

A   448 square inches   B   896 square inches

C   1,025 square inches   D   2,368 square inches

Copyright © Houghton Mifflin Company. All rights reserved.

Go On

11. Which description does NOT apply to this figure?

- Ⓐ equilateral triangle
- Ⓒ isosceles triangle
- Ⓑ right triangle
- Ⓓ acute triangle

12. Carlie plans to paint a wall that has a window. How much area will she be covering?

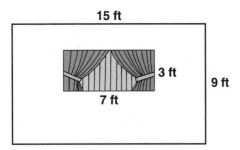

- Ⓐ 156 square feet
- Ⓒ 114 square feet
- Ⓑ 135 square feet
- Ⓓ 21 square feet

13. Which of the following transformations shows a translation?

Ⓐ M W

Ⓑ M Ɯ

Ⓒ M M

Ⓓ M
   W

Copyright © Houghton Mifflin Company. All rights reserved.

Go On

14. Which figure does NOT have line symmetry?

Ⓐ

Ⓑ

Ⓒ

Ⓓ

15. What is the volume of this figure?

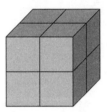

Ⓐ 1 cubic unit

Ⓑ 2 cubic units

Ⓒ 4 cubic units

Ⓓ 8 cubic units

16. What is the perimeter of this shape?

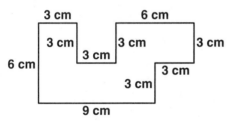

Ⓐ 18 cm Ⓑ 28 cm Ⓒ 42 cm Ⓓ 60 cm

17. Brad wants to replace the sand in his little sister's sandbox. The sandbox is 5 feet square and 1 foot deep. He wants to fill it halfway. How many cubic feet of sand will he need? Show your work.

Answer: _____

Copyright © Houghton Mifflin Company. All rights reserved.

Go On

18. Draw the following figure to show a translation. Then draw the figure to show a reflection across a horizontal line. Draw it again to show the figure rotated 180° to the right. Label each drawing with the name of the transformation.

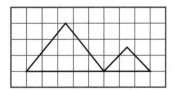

Answer:
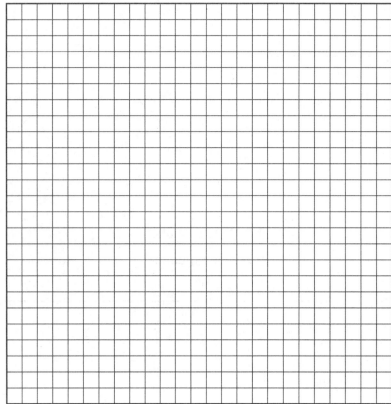

Copyright © Houghton Mifflin Company. All rights reserved.

Go On

19. This is a diagram of Angelo's rose garden. How many feet of fencing will he need to enclose it? If he wants each of his rose bushes to have 4 square feet of space, how many rose bushes can he plant? Show all your work.

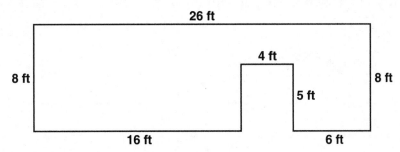

Answer: _____

_____

_____

_____

20. Keesha stores blankets in a chest that measures 36 inches by 20 inches by 20 inches. What is the surface area of the chest? What is the volume of the chest? Show all your work.

Answer: _____

_____

_____

_____

Copyright © Houghton Mifflin Company. All rights reserved.

Stop

Fill in the letter of the correct answer.

1. A bag of marbles has 20 red marbles, 20 green marbles, 40 yellow marbles, and 10 black marbles. What is the probability that you would pick out a black marble if you reached in the bag without looking?

   (A) 0   (B) $\frac{1}{9}$ (C) $\frac{1}{20}$ (D) $\frac{1}{40}$

2. Which percent is the same as $\frac{3}{5}$?

   (A) 30%   (B) 35%   (C) 53%   (D) 60%

3. Which expression does not match the others?

   (A) $\frac{4}{5}$ (B) 40%   (C) 80%   (D) 4:5

4. A drawing of a patio is made with a scale of $\frac{1}{4}$ inch:5 feet. If the patio is 50 feet wide, how wide is it in the drawing?

   (A) 50 inches   (B) 10 inches   (C) 5 inches   (D) $2\frac{1}{2}$ inches

5. How many combinations are possible if you have 10 shirts and 5 pairs of pants?

   (A) 5   (B) 10   (C) 15   (D) 50

6. Dan and Emily played 12 games of checkers. Dan won 9 of them. What percent of the games did Dan win?

   (A) 9%   (B) 12%   (C) 25%   (D) 75%

7. Danielle walks 4 miles per hour. At that rate, how long will it take her to walk 24 miles?

   (A) 6 hours   (B) 12 hours   (C) 20 hours   (D) 28 hours

Copyright © Houghton Mifflin Company. All rights reserved.

Go On

Name _____ Date _____

8. Which decimal represents the percent of his income that Patrick puts into savings?

Patrick's Income

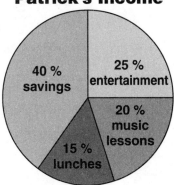

- Ⓐ 0.2
- Ⓑ 0.4
- Ⓒ 2.0
- Ⓓ 4.0

9. A total of 48 fifth-graders entered projects in the science fair. There were 12 projects related to biology. What percent of the fifth-grade participants entered projects related to biology?

- Ⓐ 48%
- Ⓑ 36%
- Ⓒ 25%
- Ⓓ 12%

10. Based on this line plot, what is the probability that a person interviewed randomly would like baseball the best?

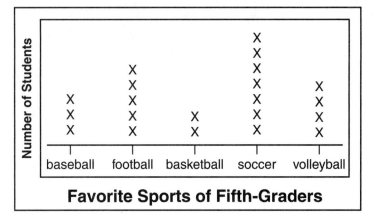

- Ⓐ $\frac{1}{21}$
- Ⓑ $\frac{1}{7}$
- Ⓒ $\frac{1}{5}$
- Ⓓ $\frac{3}{5}$

Copyright © Houghton Mifflin Company. All rights reserved.

Go On

11. Daria packed a pair of jeans, a pair of black slacks, a black skirt, and a tan skirt. She also packed a white blouse, a black sweater, a black blouse, and a green blouse. How many different outfits can she put together with these items?

(A) 4   (B) 8   (C) 16   (D) 32

---

12. Kim is using one kind of bead and one kind of sequin in each design. Which organized list shows the possible combinations she can use?

Beads	Sequins
gold	red
silver	blue
	green
	purple

(A) gold beads, red sequins
gold beads, blue sequins
gold beads, green sequins
gold beads, purple sequins
silver beads, red sequins
silver beads, blue sequins
silver beads, green sequins
silver beads, purple sequins

(B) gold beads, gold sequins
gold beads, silver sequins
green beads, green sequins
red beads, purple sequins
silver sequins, red beads
red sequins, blue beads
silver beads, green sequins
silver beads, purple sequins

(C) gold beads, red, blue, and green sequins
silver beads, red, blue, and green sequins

(D) gold beads, silver beads
red, blue, and green sequins

Copyright © Houghton Mifflin Company. All rights reserved.

Go On

13. How tall is the tree shown in the drawing?

$\frac{1}{2}$ in. : 4 ft

(A) 4 feet   (B) 12 feet   (C) 20 feet   (D) 24 feet

---

14. What is the likelihood of the spinner landing on stripes?

(A) unlikely   (B) likely   (C) certain   (D) impossible

---

15. Tim made 3 bracelets using 140 beads in all. Which of the following does NOT express the ratio of 140 beads to 3 bracelets?

(A) $\frac{3}{140}$

(B) 140 to 3

(C) 140:3

(D) $\frac{140}{3}$

Copyright © Houghton Mifflin Company. All rights reserved.

Go On

16. The ratio of students to teachers at Middlefield School is 15 to 1. If there are 600 students in the school, how many teachers are there?

(A) 4   (B) 40   (C) 45   (D) 90

17. A swimsuit manufacturer offers 15 different styles in 5 different colors. James wants to order one of each possible design for his store. How many different designs will he order? The suits come in sizes S, M, and L. If he wants 3 of each design in each size, how many will he order in all? Show all your work.

Answer: _____

_____

_____

_____

18. A survey of 200 students revealed the following data: 40 had one brother, 40 had one sister, 80 had one brother and one sister, and 40 had no siblings. Create a circle graph to display these data as percents.

Copyright © Houghton Mifflin Company. All rights reserved.

Go On

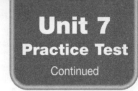
19. Caron's rate of pay is $120 a day. Sean's rate of pay is $18 per hour. If Sean works 7 hours a day for 6 days, and Caron works 6 days, who will get a bigger paycheck? How much bigger? Show your work on the lines below.

Answer: _____

_____

_____

_____

20. Dirk is on a diet of 2,000 Calories per day. Maryanne is on a diet of 1,200 Calories per day. By 4:00 P.M. Dirk had consumed 1,200 Calories, and Maryanne had consumed 900. What percent of their totals had each person consumed by 4:00 P.M.? Show your work.

Answer: _____

Copyright © Houghton Mifflin Company. All rights reserved.

Stop

Fill in the letter of the correct answer.

1. Cynthia's scores during four moves in a board game were $^+40$ points, $^-18$ points, $^+22$ points, and $^-6$ points. What was her score after those four moves?

   Ⓐ $^-24$ points

   Ⓒ $^+62$ points

   Ⓑ $^+38$ points

   Ⓓ $^+86$ points

2. What is the value of x?

   $8x + 4 = 36$

   Ⓐ $x = 4$

   Ⓒ $x = 24$

   Ⓑ $x = 8$

   Ⓓ $x = 32$

3. The table shows a relationship between exercise time (e) and Calories burned (c). Which equation describes the relationship?

Exercise Time (minutes)	20	30	40	50	60
Calories burned	200	300	400	500	600

   Ⓐ $c = 10e$

   Ⓒ $c = e \div 100$

   Ⓑ $c = e + 100$

   Ⓓ $c = 100 \div e$

4. Each of 6 music students spent the same amount of time practicing last week. They spent a total of 72 hours practicing. Which equation would help you figure out how many hours each student spent practicing?

   Ⓐ $h = 72 + 6$

   Ⓒ $h = 72 - 6$

   Ⓑ $72h = 6$

   Ⓓ $6h = 72$

Copyright © Houghton Mifflin Company. All rights reserved.

Go On

5. The table shows the cost of movie tickets. Which equation describes the relationship between the number of tickets (t) and the cost (c)?

Movie Tickets	
Tickets	**Cost**
1	$9.25
2	$18.50
3	$27.75
4	$37.00

(A) $t + \$9.25 = c$ (B) $t \times \$9.25 = c$

(C) $t - \$9.25 = c$ (D) $t \div \$9.25 = c$

6. Which number completes the number sentence?

$$^-19 - {}^-12 = \square$$

(A) $^-7$ (B) $^+7$ (C) $^-31$ (D) $^+31$

7. Six friends compared their weights before and after a given period of time. The table shows how many pounds each person gained or lost. Order the numbers from lowest to highest.

Weight Changes	
Person	**Gain or Loss**
Mary	$^+9$
Matthew	$^+13$
Simone	$^-4$
Andrew	$^-8$
Colleen	$^-3$
Jason	$^+2$

(A) $^+13, {}^+9, {}^+2, {}^-3, {}^-4, {}^-8$ (B) $^-8, {}^-4, {}^-3, {}^+2, {}^+9, {}^+13$

(C) $^+2, {}^+9, {}^+13, {}^-8, {}^-4, {}^-3$ (D) $^-3, {}^-4, {}^-8, {}^+8, {}^+4, {}^+3$

Copyright © Houghton Mifflin Company. All rights reserved.

Go On

8. Shonda's goal is to learn 20 new Spanish words a week. Which equation shows how many vocabulary words (v) Shonda will learn after a given number of weeks (w)?

  (A) $v = 20 + w$ (B) $v = w - 20$

  (C) $v = 20w$ (D) $v = w \div 20$

9. Which comparison is true?

  (A) $^+8 = {}^-8$ (B) $^+8 > {}^-8$

  (C) $^+8 < {}^-8$ (D) $^+8 < {}^-9$

Use this coordinate plane to answer Questions 10–11.

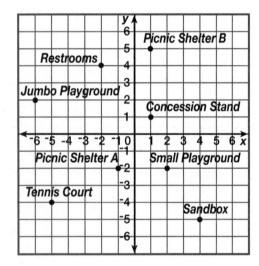

10. Kamal is at the small playground. If he moved according to a translation of down 3 followed by a right 2, where would he be?

  (A) tennis court   (B) concession stand

  (C) jumbo playground   (D) sandbox

11. Which ordered pair describes the position of the tennis court?

  (A) $^-4, {}^-5$ (B) $^+5, {}^+4$

  (C) $^-5, {}^-4$ (D) $^+4, {}^+5$

Copyright © Houghton Mifflin Company. All rights reserved.

Go On

Use this grid to answer Questions 12–13.

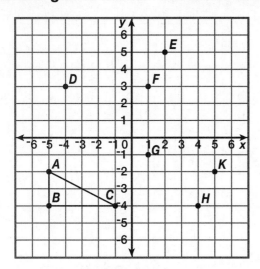

12. Which point is located at ($^+$2, $^+$5)?

   (A) E   (B) F   (C) H   (D) K

13. If triangle ABC is translated 7 units up and 7 units to the right, at
    which position will point *A* be located?

   (A) $^+$7, $^+$7   (B) $^-$7, $^-$7   (C) $^-$2, $^-$5   (D) $^+$2, $^+$5

14. What is the absolute value of $^+$18?

   (A) $^+$18   (B) $^-$18   (C) 18 − 18   (D) 18

15. What numbers would complete this function table?

| Function: $y = x + 4$ ||
x	y
$^-$2	$^+$2
$^-$1	
0	
$^+$1	

   (A) $^+$3, $^+$4, $^+$5   (B) $^-$3, $^-$4, $^-$5   (C) $^+$4, $^+$6, $^+$8   (D) $^-$4, $^-$6, $^-$8

Copyright © Houghton Mifflin Company. All rights reserved.

Go On

16. Michael mows 2 lawns per hour. Which graph shows this?

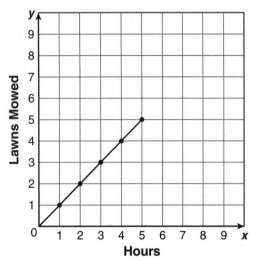

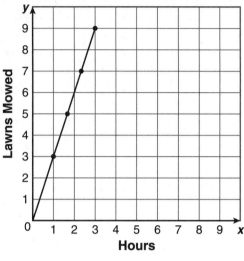

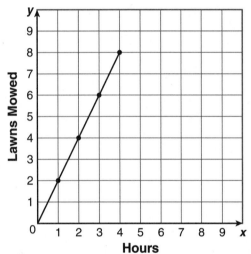

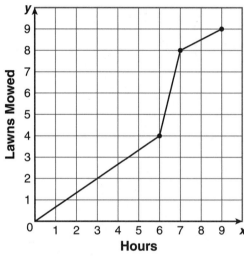

17. Mrs. Raymond pays $45 a month in gym fees. Group classes, such as aerobics and yoga, cost an extra $5 per class. Write an equation to show the total cost (*c*) of belonging to the gym and taking a given number of group classes (*g*). Use your equation to find out how much it will cost Mrs. Raymond in one month if she takes 13 group classes.

Answer: _____

_____

Copyright © Houghton Mifflin Company. All rights reserved.

Go On

18. In May Jésus borrowed $48 from his sister Angela. In June he
    borrowed another $96. In July Angela borrowed $84 from Jésus,
    and in August she borrowed another $32. By the end of August,
    who owed whom, and how much did he or she owe? Show
    all your work.

    Answer: _____

    _____

    _____

19. Plot and label each ordered pair below. Then connect points
    A to E in order, and connect point E to point A. What figure
    have you created?

    point A: (⁻4, ⁻1)
    point B: (⁻1, ⁺3)
    point C: (⁺2, ⁻1)
    point D: (⁻5, ⁺2)
    point E: (⁺3, ⁺2)

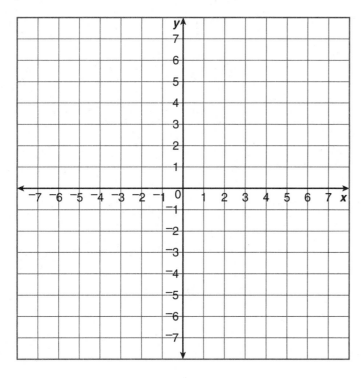

    Answer: _____

Copyright © Houghton Mifflin Company. All rights reserved.

Go On

20. The table shows the cost of getting a sweater dry-cleaned. Write and solve an equation to find out how much it would cost to get 12 sweaters dry-cleaned.

Dry Cleaning Costs

Sweaters	Price ($)
1	4
2	8
3	12

Answer: _____

_____

_____

Copyright © Houghton Mifflin Company. All rights reserved.

Stop

Answer Key
and
Scoring Rubrics

ANSWER KEY

AYP Test 1

1. C (3, 4)
2. C $2(x + 10) = 42$
3. D 8
4. B $x + 8 = 16$
5. B 24
6. C

7. A

8. D

9. C acute
10. C 10 hours
11. D rhinoceros
12. C $2\frac{1}{2}$ in.
13. C hours
14. C 135
15. C 43%
16. C 3.1 miles
17. B seventy-five hundredths
18. C 80%
19. C $8.81
20. A $1.19
21. D two-thirds
22. C 12
23. D $\frac{4}{9}$
24. B 3
25. D $31.70
26. D estimation
27. B how many weeds he pulled
28. C 10
29. A higher than the median
30. B 4 ft 1 in.
31. D 1 ft 11 in.
32. B $\frac{7}{13}$

33. Since line AB and line GH form a right angle at their intersection, then $\overleftrightarrow{AB}$ is perpendicular to $\overleftrightarrow{GH}$

34. $3 \times 9 = 27$; the perimeter is 27 centimeters

35. I; I is the letter most likely to be picked because it occurs 3 times out of 13 possible outcomes. P, R, O, A, L, T, E, S; Each letter occurs 1 time out of 13 so each letter is equally likely to be least likely picked.

36. For example: 10, 7; The second number is 3 less than the first number in each pair.

37. The figures in the 'YES' row are representations of solid figures while the figures in the 'NO' row are not (they are representations of plane figures).

38. March and May; March and May

39. 360°; 48 feet; 150.72 feet

40. $696; $(72 \times 5) + (84 \times 4) = 360 + 336 = 696$

AYP Test 2

1. B B
2. A $2n - 4$
3. B 13
4. B 20
5. C 15, 22
6. C

7. D

8. C

9. B 2 and 3
10. C year
11. C 6 lbs, 8 oz
12. C 8.5 cm
13. B centimeter

AYP Tests Questions 33 and 34 have a 1-point maximum score; Questions 35–38 have a 2-point maximum score. Questions 39 and 40 have a 4-point maximum score.

Copyright © Houghton Mifflin Company. All rights reserved.

14. C 30

15. C 5 hours

16. D $\frac{1}{6}$

17. A 0.3

18. C 3

19. C 6.06 kilowatts

20. C 3.96 kilowatts

21. C $\frac{18}{33}$

22. B 12

23. B 6.9 lbs

24. C $399.75

25. D $\frac{1}{12}$ pound

26. C 3,200 ÷ 80

27. B how many cans of oil were in each case

28. C 3

29. A 56.6 minutes

30. B 50 minutes

31. C 60 minutes

32. B $\frac{4}{10}$

33. Answers will vary. Sample answers: $\overline{AB}$ is parallel to $\overline{CD}$, $\overline{GH}$ is parallel to $\overline{IJ}$; $\overline{KG}$ is perpendicular to $\overline{GH}$, $\overline{AB}$ is perpendicular to $\overline{BL}$, $\overline{CD}$ is perpendicular to $\overline{BL}$

34. 20 inches

35. red; The spinner is most likely to land on red because red occupies the greatest number of sectors of the circle.

36. (7, 49); the first number is the next odd number after 5 and the second number is the product of the first number and 7.

37. Answers will vary. Sample answers: Polygon or not a polygon; plane figure or solid figure; figure with vertices or figure without vertices

38. 20 votes; 2 × 10 = 20

39. 180˚; 2 × 10 ft, or 20 ft; 62.8 ft

40. 336 pounds of rice; (20 × 7) + (10 × 10) + (5 × 5) + (21 × 1) = 336

AYP Test 3

1. C (1, 2)

2. C 3 · p + 6

3. C 39

4. D x ÷ 5 = 1

5. D divide by 3, multiply by 5

6. A

7. D

8. B

9. A

10. B 3 hours

11. C raisin

12. B 6.5 cm

13. D

14. A 24

15. C 13,000

16. C $\frac{3}{4}$

17. D 0.0009

18. A Mr. Martin and Mrs. Ortiz

19. A $66.85

20. B $15.71

21. C multiply bill by 0.05

22. D 15 in.

23. B $0.50

24. C $\frac{1}{2}$ of the can

25. D 15 feet

26. A 99 as 100 − 1

27. C how much the stuffed animal costs

28. D 36

29. D 33-inch club

30. C 32-inch club

31. A 7

32. B $\frac{3}{8}$

AYP Tests Questions 33 and 34 have a 1-point maximum score; Questions 35–38 have a 2-point maximum score. Questions 39 and 40 have a 4-point maximum score.

Copyright © Houghton Mifflin Company. All rights reserved.

33. $\overleftrightarrow{EH}$ is perpendicular to $\overrightarrow{FG}$

34. 24 in.; 2(7 in. + 5 in.) = 2 × 12 in. = 24 in.

35. 1 and 4; 1 and 4 are most likely to be pulled out because there are four 1s, one 2, one 3, and four 4s.

36. 5, 25; the first number is the next counting number in the column and the second number is the first number times 5.

37. Sample answers: A solid figure is represented by the first figure and a plane figure is represented by the second figure. The first figure is a prism and the second figure is a polygon. The first figure has 8 vertices and the second figure has 6 vertices.

38. 60 runs, 1st year: 4 × 12 = 48 runs; 2nd year: 2 × 12 = 24 runs; 3rd year: 3 × 12 = 36 runs; 48 + 24 + 36 = 108 runs; 168 − 108 = 60

39. 2 centimeters; 180°; 12.56 centimeters

40. 6 miles; Tom rode for a total of 30 minutes, 15 minutes to the store and then 15 minutes back to his house. 30 minutes is $\frac{1}{2}$ hour. He rode $\frac{1}{2}$ hour at 12 mph. $\frac{1}{2} × 12 = 6$

Practice Test Unit 1

1. D 940,213 *[Unit Objective 1A]*
2. A 489.3; 48.92; 4.894 *[Unit Objective 1B]*
3. A 47 + n = 50 *[Unit Objective 1C]*
4. A 2 large avocados *[Unit Objective 1D]*
5. C 19,986 acres *[Unit Objective 1E]*
6. D 24 *[Unit Objective 1F]*
7. B forty and three hundred twenty-six thousandths *[Unit Objective 1A]*
8. D 65 *[Unit Objective 1C]*
9. A 29,748 square miles *[Unit Objective 1E]*
10. B 4 *[Unit Objective 1F]*
11. B sixty thousand *[Unit Objective 1A]*
12. A 1,990,428 *[Unit Objective 1E]*
13. B 10 *[Unit Objective 1F]*
14. C 457 > 382 *[Unit Objective 1B]*
15. A 1,200 *[Unit Objective 1D]*
16. C $298.49 *[Unit Objective 1B]*
17. Golden Gate; 4,200 feet; 2,329 feet *[Unit Objective 1G]*

18. 1,250 − 853 = 397 *[Unit Objective 1G]*
19. *Jefferson* = 23
    Madison = 23 + 5 = 28
    (number at Jefferson plus 5)
    Washington = 28 + 3 = 31
    (number at Madison plus 3)
    23 + 28 + 31 = 82 (number at Jefferson plus number at Madison plus number at Washington)
    [Unit Objective 1G]
20. $40.00 − $7.61 = n
    $40.00 − $7.61 = $32.39 *[Unit Objective 1G]*

Practice Test Unit 2

1. C 192 *[Unit Objective 2C]*
2. A (5 × 10) + (5 × 3) *[Unit Objective 2A]*
3. D 240 *[Unit Objective 2B]*
4. A 7 *[Unit Objective 2D]*
5. B $4.00 *[Unit Objective 2B]*
6. D 10 (6 × 4) *[Unit Objective 2A]*
7. B 134 *[Unit Objective 2C]*
8. C 4 *[Unit Objective 2D]*
9. A 26 R26 *[Unit Objective 2C]*
10. B $8 × 50 *[Unit Objective 2B]*
11. A 15 *[Unit Objective 2D]*
12. C 32 + 9 − 18 *[Unit Objective 2E]*
13. B 8 × 14 = (8 × 10) + (8 × 4) *[Unit Objective 2A]*
14. A 0 *[Unit Objective 2E]*
15. B 6 *[Unit Objective 2C]*
16. D 2 *[Unit Objective 2E]*
17. 19 cars will have to be completely filled. The 20th car will be partially filled when Justine gets a seat in the 20th car. 155 ÷ 8 = 19 R3 *[Unit Objective 2F]*
18. He'll have to work about 40 hours. By rounding $238 to $240, it's easy to divide it by 6 to get 40. *[Unit Objective 2F]*
19. 3d = 45, *so* d = 15
    Dave planted 15 pansies.
    45 + 15 = 60
    They planted 60 pansies in all.
    [Unit Objective 2F]

Practice Tests Questions 17 and 18 each have a 2-point maximum score; Questions 19 and 20 each have a 4-point maximum score.

Copyright © Houghton Mifflin Company. All rights reserved.

20. $5n + 4n = 126$

$9n = 126$

$n = 14$

If $n = 14$, then $5n$ (the number of rock-and-roll CDs) = 70

If $n = 14$, then $4n$ (the number of jazz CDs) = 56

[Unit Objective 2F]

Practice Test Unit 3

1. C 9 *[Unit Objective 3D]*

2. B 7 *[Unit Objective 3D]*

3. B 200 milliliters *[Unit Objective 3A]*

4. A 12 *[Unit Objective 3B]*

5. C $4\frac{3}{4}$ inches *[Unit Objective 3A]*

6. C

[Unit Objective 3B]

7. C 100 *[Unit Objective 3A]*

8. A 14 degrees *[Unit Objective 3B]*

9. D

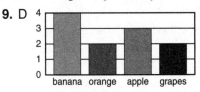

[Unit Objective 3C]

10. D line graph *[Unit Objective 3D]*

11. C 86 *[Unit Objective 3A]*

12. B 84 *[Unit Objective 3D]*

13. C double line graph *[Unit Objective 3C]*

14. B 35 years *[Unit Objective 3E]*

15. D gorilla and horse *[Unit Objective 3E]*

16. C 20 years *[Unit Objective 3E]*

17. 4,100 gallons. Possible explanation:

2 bottles = 32 ounces = 1 quart

4 quarts = 1 gallon, so 8 bottles = 8 gallons

32,800 gallons ÷ 8 = 4,100 gallons

[Unit Objective 3F]

18. Possible explanation: Dennis's graph is misleading because the dollar amounts do not increase in equal increments. A better graph would be as follows. *[Unit Objective 3F]*

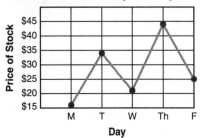

19. Dena: 4 feet, 11 inches; Albert: 4 feet, 4 inches; Jacob: 4 feet 1 inches; Tiffany: 3 feet, 11 inches; Lavonne: 4 feet, 7 inches

In order from tallest to shortest: Dena, Lavonne, Albert, Jacob, Tiffany *[Unit Objective 3D]*

20.

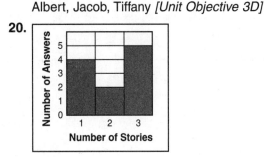

mode = 3

range = 2

Practice Test Unit 4

1. C 11 *[Unit Objective 4A]*

2. D $\frac{2}{3}$ $\frac{12}{18}$ *[Unit Objective 4C]*

3. A 15 *[Unit Objective 4B]*

4. A $8.00 *[Unit Objective 4E]*

5. C 54 *[Unit Objective 4B]*

6. B 2 *[Unit Objective 4A]*

7. D $\frac{3}{4}$ *[Unit Objective 4C]*

8. C $6\frac{3}{8}$ *[Unit Objective 4D]*

9. D $48.61 *[Unit Objective 4G]*

10. D $3\frac{4}{5}$ *[Unit Objective 4D]*

11. D about 9 miles *[Unit Objective 4E]*

12. B 6 *[Unit Objective 4B]*

13. A $15\frac{5}{8}$ *[Unit Objective 4F]*

14. A 0.48, $\frac{1}{3}$, 0.3, $\frac{1}{9}$ *[Unit Objective 4D]*

Practice Tests Questions 17 and 18 each have a 2-point maximum score; Questions 19 and 20 each have a 4-point maximum score.

Copyright © Houghton Mifflin Company. All rights reserved.

15. B $1\frac{3}{8}$ yards *[Unit Objective 4F]*

16. B 6.1842 *[Unit Objective 4G]*

17. The difference is $2\frac{3}{4}$; $6\frac{3}{8}$ has to be changed to $5\frac{11}{8}$ so $3\frac{5}{8}$ can be subtracted from it. The result is $2\frac{6}{8}$, which in its simplest form is $2\frac{3}{4}$. *[Unit Objective 4H]*

18. \$229.61; \$1,062.40 *[Unit Objective 4H]*

19. The greatest number of gift bags Michael can make is 8. Each bag will have 7 pens and 9 toy cars. *[Unit Objective 4H]*

20. 24 pounds *[Unit Objective 4H]*

3.7	=	$3\frac{7}{10}$	=	$3\frac{70}{100}$
8.75	=	$8\frac{75}{100}$	=	$8\frac{75}{100}$
4.3	=	$4\frac{3}{10}$	=	$4\frac{30}{100}$
7.25	=	$7\frac{25}{100}$	=	$7\frac{25}{100}$
24.00		$22\frac{200}{100}$	=	24

Practice Test Unit 5

1. C 36 *[Unit Objective 5A]*

2. B 4 *[Unit Objective 5B]*

3. D 0.06 × 0.06 *[Unit Objective 5C]*

4. B 4 *[Unit Objective 5A]*

5. B 3 *[Unit Objective 5B]*

6. C 30 mi/gal *[Unit Objective 5B]*

7. D 6 days *[Unit Objective 5A]*

8. A $1\frac{1}{4}$ cups *[Unit Objective 5A]*

9. C 54.3 ÷ 3 > 98.4 ÷ 6 *[Unit Objective 5C]*

10. C 28.4347 *[Unit Objective 5C]*

11. D 96 square feet *[Unit Objective 5C]*

12. C 80 *[Unit Objective 5B]*

13. B \$14.67 *[Unit Objective 5C]*

14. D 14 *[Unit Objective 5A]*

15. B 12.0625 *[Unit Objective 5C]*

16. D 0.4 *[Unit Objective 5B]*

17. 60 × 0.35 = 21 people came to the party; 60 − 21 = 39 people failed to show up *[Unit Objective 5D]*

18. $1\frac{1}{4} \times 3 = 3\frac{3}{4}$; $3\frac{3}{4} \div 12 = \frac{15}{4} \times \frac{1}{12} = \frac{5}{16}$ cup *[Unit Objective 5D]*

19. Basil's walking speed is faster.

Jan: $23\frac{2}{5} \div 9 = \frac{117}{5} \times \frac{1}{9} = \frac{13}{5} = 2\frac{3}{5}$ mi/h

Basil: $12\frac{3}{4} \div 4\frac{1}{4} = \frac{51}{4} \times \frac{4}{17} = 3$

[Unit Objective 5D]

20. Katie's hourly wage is greater by \$0.50.

Katie: \$292.50 ÷ 26 = \$11.25

Brett: \$354.75 ÷ 33 = \$10.75

\$11.25 − \$10.75 = \$0.50 *[Unit Objective 5D]*

Practice Test Unit 6

1. A 36 feet *[Unit Objective 6D]*

2. D pentagon *[Unit Objective 6A]*

3. A

[Unit Objective 6B]

4. A 59.66 mm *[Unit Objective 6E]*

5. B

[Unit Objective 6B]

6. B He could use the letter "b" and change it by a reflection across a vertical line. *[Unit Objective 6C]*

7. D 94.2 inches *[Unit Objective 6E]*

8. D E

[Unit Objective 6C]

9. B 54 square feet *[Unit Objective 6D]*

10. D 2,368 square inches *[Unit Objective 6F]*

11. B right triangle *[Unit Objective 6A]*

12. C 114 square feet *[Unit Objective 6D]*

13. C **M M**

[Unit Objective 6C]

14. B

[Unit Objective 6B]

15. D 8 cubic units *[Unit Objective 6F]*

16. C 42 cm *[Unit Objective 6D]*

Practice Tests Questions 17 and 18 each have a 2-point maximum score; Questions 19 and 20 each have a 4-point maximum score.

Copyright © Houghton Mifflin Company. All rights reserved.

17. 5 ft × 5 ft × 0.5 ft = 12.5 cubic feet of sand
[Unit Objective 6G]

18. translation:

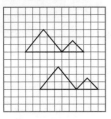

reflection across a horizontal line:

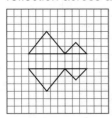

rotation of 180° to the right:

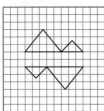

[Unit Objective 6G]

19. 26 + 8 + 6 + 5 + 4 + 5 + 16 + 8 = 78 feet of fencing

26 × 8 = 208 − 20 = 188 square feet

188 ÷ 4 = 47 rose bushes *[Unit Objective 6G]*

20. 36 × 20 = 720 × 4 surfaces = 2,880 square inches; 20 × 20 = 400 × 2 surfaces = 800 square inches; 2,880 + 800 = 3,680 square inches

36 × 20 × 20 = 14,400 cubic inches *[Unit Objective 6G]*

Practice Test Unit 7

1. B $\frac{1}{9}$ *[Unit Objective 7F]*

2. D 60% *[Unit Objective 7D]*

3. B 40% *[Unit Objective 7C]*

4. D $2\frac{1}{2}$ inches *[Unit Objective 7B]*

5. D 50 *[Unit Objective 7E]*

6. D 75% *[Unit Objective 7C]*

7. A 6 hours *[Unit Objective 7A]*

8. B 0.4 *[Unit Objective 7C]*

9. C 25% *[Unit Objective 7D]*

10. B $\frac{1}{7}$ *[Unit Objective 7F]*

11. C 16 *[Unit Objective 7E]*

12. A gold beads, red sequins
gold beads, blue sequins
gold beads, green sequins
gold beads, purple sequins
silver beads, red sequins
silver beads, blue sequins
silver beads, green sequins
silver beads, purple sequins
[Unit Objective 7E]

13. C 20 feet *[Unit Objective 7B]*

14. B likely *[Unit Objective 7F]*

15. A $\frac{3}{140}$ *[Unit Objective 7A]*

16. B 40 *[Unit Objective 7A]*

17. 15 × 5 = 75 different designs

75 × 3 = 225 suits × 3 sizes = 675 suits in all *[Unit Objective 7G]*

18.

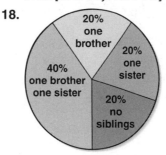

[Unit Objective 7G]

19. Caron: $120 × 6 = $720

Sean: $18 × 7 × 6 = $756

Sean's paycheck will be bigger by $36. *[Unit Objective 7G]*

20. Dirk: $\frac{1200}{2000} = \frac{12}{20} = \frac{6}{10} = 60\%$

Maryanne: $\frac{900}{1200} = \frac{9}{12} = \frac{3}{4} = 75\%$

[Unit Objective 7G]

Copyright © Houghton Mifflin Company. All rights reserved.

Practice Tests Questions 17 and 18 each have a 2-point maximum score; Questions 19 and 20 each have a 4-point maximum score.

Practice Test Unit 8

1. B +38 points *[Unit Objective 8D]*

2. A x = 4 *[Unit Objective 8A]*

3. A c = 10e *[Unit Objective 8B]*

4. D 6h = 72 *[Unit Objective 8A]*

5. B t × $9.25 = c *[Unit Objective 8B]*

6. A −7 *[Unit Objective 8D]*

7. B −8, −4, −3, +2, +9, +13 *[Unit Objective 8C]*

8. C v = 20w *[Unit Objective 8A]*

9. B +8 > −8 *[Unit Objective 8C]*

10. D sandbox *[Unit Objective 8G]*

11. C −5, −4 *[Unit Objective 8E]*

12. A E *[Unit Objective 8E]*

13. D +2, +5 *[Unit Objective 8G]*

14. D 18 *[Unit Objective 8C]*

15. A +3, +4, +5 *[Unit Objective 8F]*

16. C
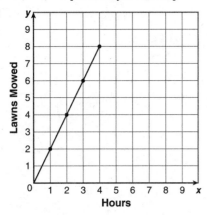

[Unit Objective 8F]

17. c = $45 + $5g; c = $45 + ($5 × 13) = $45 + $65 = $110 *[Unit Objective 8H]*

18. Jésus borrowed $48 + $96 = $144; Angela borrowed $84 + $32 = $116.

    $144 − $116 = $28; Jésus owes Angela $28.
    [Unit Objective 8H]

19. A star

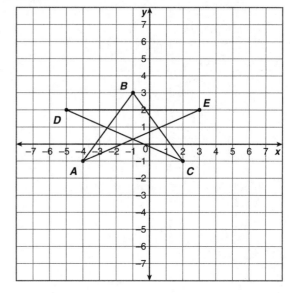

[Unit Objective 8H]

20. c = 4s

    c = (4 × 12)

    c = $48 *[Unit Objective 8H]*

Practice Tests Questions 17 and 18 each have a 2-point maximum score; Questions 19 and 20 each have a 4-point maximum score.

— 94 —

Copyright © Houghton Mifflin Company. All rights reserved.

4-Point Rubric for Extended Constructed-Response Questions

4   **A 4-point response:** The correct answer is given; if the work needs to be shown, then the work is complete and shows thorough understanding of the concepts.
    OR
The student answers all parts completely and correctly.

3   **A 3-point response:** The correct answer is given; if the work needs to be shown, then the work is mostly complete and shows good understanding of the concepts.
    OR
A minor miscalculation leads to an incorrect answer; however, the work is complete and shows thorough understanding of the concepts.
    OR
The student answers most parts completely and correctly; one part is incomplete, incorrect or not attempted.

2   **A 2-point response:** The correct answer is given; if the work needs to be shown, then the work is partially complete and shows some understanding of the concepts.
    OR
A major miscalculation leads to an incorrect answer; however, the work is complete and shows thorough understanding of the concepts.
    OR
The student answers about half of the parts completely and correctly; about half of the parts are incomplete, incorrect or not attempted.

1   **A 1-point response:** The correct answer is given; if the work needs to be shown, then the work is incomplete and shows little understanding of the concepts.
    OR
An incorrect answer is given, and the work is complete; however, the work shows some understanding of the concepts.
    OR
The student answers only one of the parts correctly, the remaining parts are incomplete, incorrect or not attempted.

0   **A 0-point response:** The work was not attempted; shows little or no understanding of the concept.
    OR
The student does not completely and correctly answer any of the parts.

Copyright © Houghton Mifflin Company. All rights reserved.

2-Point Rubric for Short Constructed-Response Questions

2	**A 2-point response:** The correct answer is given; if the work needs to be shown, then the work is complete and shows thorough understanding of the concepts. **OR** The student answers all parts completely and correctly.
1	**A 1-point response:** The correct answer is given; if the work needs to be shown, then the work is at least partially complete and shows some understanding of the concepts. **OR** A minor miscalculation leads to an incorrect answer; however, the work is complete and shows thorough understanding of the concepts. **OR** The student answers half of the parts completely and correctly; half of the parts are incomplete, incorrect or not attempted.
0	**A 0-point response:** The work was not attempted or shows little or no understanding of the concept. **OR** The student does not completely and correctly answer any of the parts.

1 Point Rubric for Short Constructed-Response Questions

1	**A 1-point response:** The correct answer is given; if the work needs to be shown, then the work is complete and shows thorough understanding of the concepts.
0	**A 0-point response:** The work was not attempted or shows little or no understanding of the concept.

Copyright © Houghton Mifflin Company. All rights reserved.